Youth Ministry

the new team approach

Ginny Ward Holderness

Photographs by Mark Hames

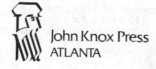

John Knox Press
ATLANTA

Unless otherwise noted, Scripture quotations are from the Revised Standard Version Bible, copyright 1946, 1952, and © 1971, 1973 by the Division of Christian Education, National Council of the Churches of Christ in the U.S.A., and used by permission.

Acknowledgement is made for permission to quote from the following: *Breaking Free* (1971), *Encyclopedia of Serendipity* (1976), *Groups in Action* (1972), *Handbook of Serendipity* (1976), and *Serendipity* (1972). All are in the Serendipity series by Lyman Coleman and used by permission of Serendipity House, Box 1012, Littleton, Colorado 80160.

Library of Congress Cataloging in Publication Data
Holderness, Ginny Ward, 1946–
   Youth ministry.

   Bibliography: p.
   Includes index.
   1. Church work with youth. 2. Church work with young adults. 3. Group ministry. I. Title.
BV4447.H64   259'.23   80-82186
ISBN 0-8042-1410-7

©copyright John Knox Press 1981
10 9 8 7 6 5 4 3
Printed in the United States of America
John Knox Press
Atlanta, Georgia

Foreword

Reading *Youth Ministry: The New Team Approach* brought nostalgic memories of good days in youth ministry at Grace Covenant Presbyterian Church in Richmond some years ago when we had a team of ten people, five youth and five adults, serving together. A youth and an adult worked in an area of responsibility. The format was somewhat different from the one explicated in this new book, obviously, but it had many of the benefits Ginny Holderness describes—team spirit, shared responsibility that did not overburden any one person, strategies for moving from a core group to involving everyone, including parents, plans made in advance for a long period of time, to offer only a few examples. Like Ginny, I wrote and taught out of my experience, with gratitude for the gift of friendship with youth and adults who shared in dreams and in hard work.

The reason I mention this memory is that I find in *Youth Ministry: The New Team Approach* a work that will help *many* groups experience the kind of rewards I have just described. It is a plan appropriate for today; it is tested; it is filled with specific, clear guidelines. Not only that, but we have offered here a wealth of ideas and resources, all organized in such a way that one can find and work with them quickly and easily. The kind of vitality and creativity I knew in Ginny as a student is functioning at full capacity, disciplined, made available to others through work, experience, and clear thinking. She offers an excellent book for both junior high and senior high leaders, a companion and supplement to *The Exuberant Years,* with its focus on junior highs.

Recently a friend of mine, a capable analyst of education and of culture, said he knew of no greater area of need than work with youth—in society generally, in education, and in youth ministry. Ginny Ward Holderness is doing something about the need, and helping others do something about it. It is for that reason I am glad to write this Foreword. It was my privilege to write one for Ginny's first work, *The Exuberant Years,* when she was a "new" writer. What I want to do here—she certainly does not need an introduction anymore—is to say that it is an honor to endorse the ideas and the approach of my colleague and friend, Ginny, and to express appreciation for *her* ministry.

—Sara P. Little
Robert and Lucy Reynolds Critz Professor of Christian Education
Union Theological Seminary, Richmond, Virginia
February 1980

Introduction

Coming back from a workshop on youth ministry, a somewhat enthusiastic and somewhat disillusioned senior high advisor remarked: "At workshops like these I always get excited about what the church could be doing in youth ministry, and then when I get home I never can figure out how to take what I have learned and develop the kind of youth program we talked about at the conference. All these good ideas will fade in a few weeks. Nothing will come of it."

Comments like this are more frequent than I would like to admit. If you have ever been to a training event, you know what I mean. The dream of having a fantastic youth group is there in the classroom, but just try to take that dream home and make it come true.

I have been teaching the approach proposed in this book at many of these events. The responses of lay leaders, ministers, and directors of Christian education have been affirming. But I see the need to give them something tangible to take home for use in developing a youth ministry. And so—another book. Like *The Exuberant Years,* this book will explain this new approach in great detail, describing every step and including all anybody would need to know to use it in the local church.

The adult leadership team concept was in the experimental state for two years prior to the writing of the manuscript. Once I began writing, I sent copies of each chapter to three field-testing situations: a large church in Shreveport, Louisiana; a medium-sized church in Birmingham, Alabama; and a small church in Altamonte Springs, Florida.

The job of field testers was to identify places where the manuscript was unclear and to ask questions which could be answered before going to press. My desire was to anticipate your questions and answer them throughout the book.

As a result of the field testing, I have found it necessary to suggest ways of adapting this approach to your local situation. One hazard with using a "step-by-step" process is that one might get the impression that this approach is too "packaged"; that is, you have to do it one way or else. So as you read, please do not interpret the process as being rigid. If you are new to youth work and need "step-by-step," you will find it here. But allow yourself the freedom, especially after you get your feet wet, to modify and adapt anywhere along the way.

I am grateful to a lot of folks who bought into this concept with enthusiasm and worked with me at different stages in putting this book together: Herb Gale, associate minister at Shelby Presbyterian Church and senior high coordinator; Myra Miller, lay leader and junior high coordinator; Suzette Kincer, director of Christian education at First Presbyterian Church in Shreveport, Louisiana; Leah Langridge, part-time youth director at St. Mark's Presbyterian Church in Altamonte Springs, Florida; and Terry Newland, associate minister at Shades Valley Presbyterian Church in Birmingham, Alabama.

Many thanks to the following list of dedicated youth leaders who all were at some point members of the youth ministry team here at Shelby Presbyterian Church (a 550-member church):

Sarah Allen	Greg Horne
Ed Blake	Wanda Horne
Janice Blake	Margaret Jackson
Bill Brooks	Watt Jackson
Carolyn Brooks	Mike Kennedy
Karen Chrisawn	Mabel Lampley
Mike Chrisawn	Bud Leopard
Barbara Dixon	Sandy Leopard
Sid Dixon	Dottie McIntyre
Buddy Dodrill	Debbie Miller
Theresa Dodrill	Jessi Ogburn
George Doggett	Joe Ogburn
Susan Doggett	Ed Patterson
Bill Drumwright	Edna Patterson
Beth Gilbert	Don Peeler
Pete Gilbert	Ginger Peeler
Larry Greer	Eleanor Pruden
Diane Hames	Connie Taylor
Mark Hames	Paul Taylor
Dale Hamrick	B.J. Wall
Jim Holderness	Steve Wall
Frank Holsenbeck	Jackie Weathers
Loi Holsenbeck	

A great big thanks to all of you who challenged me, supported and pushed me in many youth ministry workshops across the country.

Thanks: to my family—Jim, J.B., and Lorinda, and to all the Shelby junior and senior highs, without whom youth ministry would not be possible.

Contents

Section A—Introduction to the Approach

1. The Youth Ministry Team Approach   10
2. Why Youth Ministry? A Theological Frame of Reference   19
3. Getting Started   25
4. Coordinators' Chapter   28
5. Leaders' Chapter   35
6. Recruiting   48

Section B—The Process

7. The Team Begins   54
8. Meeting the Youth   57
9. Involving Parents   62
10. The Planning Retreat   68
11. Follow-up to the Planning Retreat   80
12. Throughout the Year   83
13. Adapting to Varieties of Situations   88
14. Moving into the Second Year   93

Section C—Building Leadership

15. Youth as Leaders   98
16. Leadership Training Sessions   103
17. Youth Ministry Resources   112

Appendices

A. Difference Between This Book and *The Exuberant Years*   118
B. Idea Lists Under Each of the Five Categories   120
C. Group-Building Activities   125
D. Five-Category Index to *Idealog* and *Strategies*   134

Notes   140
Index   141

Section A

Introduction to the Approach

1
The Youth Ministry
Team Approach

"We're still having problems with our youth program. We think we have a good advisor and then poof, he's gone; he quits. Says it's too much for one person. Says he's not getting any support from the church, from the minister, not even from parents. But we gave him lots of resources, new ones. Good stuff. He had a terrific program planned for this year. The youth were involved in a variety of activities. I saw their calendar. They were having special worship services which they had designed themselves. They were doing things with adults and children in the congregation. Had lots of projects and service activities. They had interesting studies and even a beach trip, a ski trip, progressive dinners, canoeing, and rough camping. It looked like the best youth program we would ever have."

What went wrong? Exactly what the youth advisor said: "It's too much for one person." That is one reason why it is getting harder and harder to find adults to work with either group—senior or junior highs. We burn them out too fast. Every Sunday night plus a few weekends for retreats, trips, and camping. That's asking a lot of one person, even two people.

At this writing *The Exuberant Years* has been around for four years. The planning process described in that book has been well received in many churches. Many have related to me the effectiveness of the balanced program concept for building a solid youth ministry.

Briefly let me explain the balanced program concept from *The Exuberant Years*. The goal of the approach is *that all youth be involved in the total life of the congregation.* In order to accomplish this goal, the youth plan three or four activities in each of the following categories:

Worship—experiences of worship as a group or with the entire congregation.

Study—the exploration of topics and issues, minicourses on various subjects, Bible study.

Ministry Within the Congregation—all that the youth do with and for older and younger members of the congregation.

Service (to the community)—youth being of service to those outside their own congregation.

Fellowship—everything else: recreation, socials, eating out, retreats, trips, group building.

The emphasis is on balance. Many youth programs are heavy on Fellowship and Study, and are lacking in the other three areas. It is in these other three areas (Worship, Ministry Within the Congregation, and Service) that youth can have opportunities to be a part of their predominantly adult congregation—an important part.

Youth are no longer seen as "them," the young people over there in their own little corner—our future church. No, they are "us," definitely part of us, the present church. In affirmation of the fact that youth are full members of our congregation, there is all the more reason to fight for youth involvement in ministry, in service, in the total life of the congregation.

The recurring objection I have received to this balanced program concept is that it is too much for one person. One of the following usually happens: (1) the adult leader resigns before the year is over; (2) he or she cancels several of the activities (just cannot do it all); (3) the advisor is exhausted and announces that youth group is breaking for the summer on April 30; or (4) the burned out leader sticks it out to the bitter end and swears he or she will never take a youth group again.

Some churches get smart and suggest that the advisor recruit a partner to swap Sundays and several folks to help with retreats and special events. Still you are likely to have a tired-of-youth youth leader.

What is all this doing to the youth? If they are fortunate enough not to be stuck all year with a leader they don't like, they still sense the overworked adult getting short on energy, temper, etc.

After hearing these complaints and being pooped myself managing a loaded calendar of youth activities, I decided something needed to be done. It all began when I was talking with a Tampa, Florida Methodist minister named Larry Green who had ten enthusiastic adults working with his senior highs. They shared responsibility, supported each other, and were not overwhelmed with a large commitment of time.

The wheels began to turn, and I saw how nicely a multi-adult team would fit with the five category system. The more I worked on the idea, the more I saw all kinds of advantages for the youth, for the adult leaders, and for the congregation.

The Youth Ministry Team Approach

The purpose is still:

> To involve *all* youth
> in the total life of the congregation

Each youth group has its own coordinator, thus a junior high coordinator and a senior high coordinator. Each group has two adults working in each of the five categories. There will be two adults working with senior highs in Worship, another two adults working in Study, and so on.

Same set-up for the junior highs. For Fellowship I recommend recruiting three or four adults instead of two. Fellowship includes recreation, retreats, special events. Since extra adults are needed for retreats and such, it seems logical to have two extra in that category.

What you have is a ten-to-twelve-adult leadership team for each youth group, a likely twenty to twenty-four adults involved in youth ministry at your church. At first glance one might say: "Hey, wait a minute! That's more adults than we have kids. They'll overwhelm

them." True, they would, if all adults were attending every youth meeting. But they won't be. At the beginning of the year, let's say late September, the adults and the youth will plan out their entire year (preferably at a retreat). At that time activities will be chosen in all five categories and placed on the calendar. The adult leaders will be responsible only for the three or four activities in their area. Once the calendar is set, the adults will know exactly when they will be working with the youth. On any given Sunday night there will be only two adults with the youth group.

A look at a sample calendar might give you a clearer picture of the leadership team approach:

September 9—Cookout and orientation for leadership

    11, 13—Leadership training (*see chapter 16*)

        16—Parent and youth get-together

    17, 20—Leadership training

        23—Cookout for senior highs and leadership
             Cookout for junior highs and leadership

    29-30—Planning retreat—senior high
            Planning retreat—junior high

October 7—Follow-up planning meeting—senior high
            Follow-up planning meeting—junior high

December 2—Leadership team meeting

January 6—Calendar check—a social event for all leaders and youth, to check calendar, rearrange if need be

March 2—Leadership team meeting (among other things, need to know at this meeting who will stay on another year, and who would like to change categories)

May 13—Spring get-together for all youth and leadership

All the leaders are involved in the September orientation, cookout, parents' night, cookout with youth, training sessions, and the planning retreat and follow-up meeting. It is essential that leaders receive not only training but also support. A solid month of team building is necessary in order to give each adult an opportunity to get on board and feel that he or she is an important part of this ministry. Ownership in the program and enthusiasm won't come without this team development.

On the following page is an actual calendar of events of a junior high youth group. The following choices of activities were made in each category by the youth at the planning retreat:

Worship: drama for church school, banner making, worship workshop

Junior High Calendar

Dates	Program	Adult Leaders	Responsible Persons
Oct. 2	Planning retreat		
9	Follow-up meeting		
15	Horseback riding	Taylors, Walls	Lauren Jackson, Andrienne Thompson, Meredith Phifer
16	Meet at church at 6:00 P.M. Eat at Burger King. Back to church to plan Halloween party.	Theresa, Jackie	
23	INSIGHT film	Barbara, Martha	
30	Halloween party for children (4-6:00 P.M.). After supper UNICEF trick or treating.	Theresa, Jackie / Debbie, Frank	Bennette Lattimore, Meredith Phifer, Carol Moss / Jon Pharr, Harvey Hamrick, Chuck Lampley
Nov. 5	Hayride	Taylors, Walls	Harvey Hamrick, Jon Pharr, Bennette Lattimore
6 / 13 / 20 / 27	Identity mini-course	Barbara, Martha	Kirby Phifer, Bonnie Wilkison, Bennette Lattimore
Dec. 4	Drama rehearsal		
11	Drama rehearsal	Myra, Bill	Lauren Jackson, Kirby Phifer, Bonnie Wilkison
18	Drama presentation for the church school		
25	Christmas (no meeting)		
Jan. 1	No meeting		
8 / 15 / 22 / 29	Mini-course on Youth Problems	Barbara, Martha	Laura Arrowood, Neal Fesperman, Calvin Smith
Feb. 3-4	Ski trip	Taylors, Walls	Chuck Lampley, Laura Arrowood, Neal Fesperman
5 / 12	Plan Fun Night	Theresa, Jackie	Andrienne Thompson, Carol Moss, Bennette Lattimore
15	Fun Night for congregational supper		
19	Banner making	Myra, Bill	Jon Pharr, Chuck Lampley, Harvey Hamrick
26	Banner making		
Mar. 5	Banner making		
12	Prepare baskets and toys	Frank, Debbie	Ruth Whetstone, Neal Fesperman, Julie Yates
19	Distribute baskets and toys		
26	Easter (no meeting)		
Apr. 1	Clean up yard	Frank, Debbie	Catherine Brant, Carol Moss, Julie Yates
2	INSIGHT film	Barbara, Martha	
9 / 16 / 23 / 30	Mini-course on Christian Denominations	Barbara, Martha	Laura Arrowood, Chuck Lampley, Lauren Jackson
May 5-6	Rough camping	Taylors, Walls	Kirby Phifer, Lauren Jackson, Bonnie Wilkison
7 / 14	Worship workshop	Myra, Bill	Meredith Phifer, Andrienne Thompson, Calvin Smith
21	Evaluation of the year		
28	Picnic		

Study: insight film, identity mini-course, youth problems, Christian churches (denominations)

Ministry Within Congregation: Halloween party for children, fun night for church supper, party for elementary children

Service: UNICEF trick/treat, baskets and toys for tots at Easter, clean up yard

Fellowship: horseback riding, hayride, ski trip, rough camping, recreation

Look at the calendar. The leaders' names for each activity are in the center. Responsible persons' (youth volunteers) names are on the right. See how the activities are spread out. Check for balance. Pick out a leader's name. Take note of his or her responsibility throughout the year. How often is he or she with the youth? (See page 82 for another example.)

The Rationale for This Approach

1) *It is too much for one person.* This was mentioned before but bears repeating. Every church wants a successful youth program. When we face the fact that a successful youth program is too much for one person, then we start to look for alternatives. The adult leadership team is an alternative. With ten or twelve adults working with the youth, there is the possibility of having a balanced, active youth ministry, with youth involved in all areas of the church's life. With ten or twelve adults you can have variety and a calendar full of activities, thus, a very active youth group.

2) *The church needs to say (and say by its actions) that youth ministry is important.* We have been saying for years that we need to find ways for more of our adult congregation to be involved in the youth program. But how? This approach offers a possible twenty-four adults plus two coordinators, twenty-six adults actively involved in the youth program. And each adult has a defined responsibility. Word will get around from these twenty-six that something is happening at our church in the area of youth.

Youth need to be visible in the life of the church, not relegated to a corner of the church school wing. With a variety of activities, especially those in Worship and Ministry Within the Congregation, the youth will be seen. This concept may seem ambitious; but an ambitious approach to youth programming may be just what our churches need in order to say that youth ministry is important!

3) *Youth need to feel like they are a part of the congregation and not "junior members."* I have worked with many young people who did not know any adults in their church, with the exception of their friends' parents and their church school teachers. Youth don't know the church board members. They don't know the dedicated women who visit the sick and bake pies for newcomers. They don't even know which members have been there for years. No wonder youth feel alienated from the church.

I must mention the exceptions found in many of the smaller churches, those under 125 members. A beauty of the small church is the way it fosters community. Responsibilities and activities are often shared among youth and adults. There are so few of any age group that intergenerational activities become the norm.

4) *Youth need to know that adults do care about them.* Adults in the church are in a unique position to have special relationships with youth. They are not authority figures as are school teachers. Church adults need not be disciplinarians. Nor are they the parents of the youth. Thus, there is a certain freedom, not found elsewhere, for these adults to be open, caring, friendly in a special way.

In this system youth have opportunities to build relationships with several adults. There's a good chance that out of twelve adults, a youth will relate well to one of them. That relationship could be one of the most important relationships in that young person's life. Think back to your own experience as a young person in the church. Was there a significant adult who influenced you in your relation to the church?

Just seeing twelve adults enthusiastic about working with their group says something very positive to the youth. They can see that adults do care. Contrast this picture with the one of the church whose church school superintendent is telling the kids in late October: "We're still trying to find an advisor for you."

There are distinct advantages in using this model, benefiting the adults, the church, and the kids.

Benefits to the Adults Involved

1) *Less intensive commitment of time.* Many adults would like to say yes when recruited to be youth leaders but cannot give that much time. And it is the conscientious, caring adult who says, "I don't want to take this on and do a sloppy job. It's not fair to the kids." I would prefer that an adult respond in this way rather than agree to do it and then not give it the needed time and energy.

In the leadership team approach we are expecting a commitment—definitely—a commitment of faith, energy, enthusiasm, caring. We want adults who like youth and want to be with them, who want to see youth experience a rich ministry and a positive relationship to the church.

The only way we can expect this kind of commitment is to ask for a lesser commitment of time. In other words, we want a quality, not a quantity, time commitment. No one can be expected to keep up a high level of enthusiasm towards youth while he or she is being worn out physically and mentally.

2) *Fellowship of team members.* Just exactly how much time, how many adult team meetings there should be during the year is left to each church and its individual situation. Many team members have come up to me after the initial cookout and expressed that they had so much fun with this new gathering of adults— why spoil it by bringing in the youth? They are being facetious . . . I hope . . . at least, a little. I like what they are saying. Being coordinator is rewarding when you see your adult team enjoying each other.

Each time I have broken in a new leadership team, I have seen enthusiasm build during the frequent September sessions. In fact, by the time the last training session is over, I have had to caution them not to be too disappointed when they actually get together with the youth. Sounds ridiculous, but it's true. The anticipation of this new program builds. So the adults need to be warned that the youth are not necessarily going to be all that enthusiastic, especially in the beginning. This is new to them. Some youth will be skeptical. And there may be the exceptionally antagonistic kid who will try to sabotage the system, just for the fun of it.

3) *This model draws on the talents and interests of each individual adult leader.* When we recruit leaders for the leadership team, we ask them where their interests are with youth. We find some adults who love to go camping, skiing, canoeing, but would panic if they had to lead a study. Fine. They are the ones we want in the Fellowship area. Then there is the woman who can't stand recreation, but has some skills in using a variety of methods for mini-courses. We recruit her for the Study area. There are church members who are actively involved in the community and would like to help youth find service opportunities. Perfect people for Service.

In the old system we recruited leaders and expected them to do it all. They were to lead studies, find service projects, work with the kids on youth worship services, and lead recreation. Of course, what happened was the youth got to do only what the leaders would do. Those advisors who couldn't lead a study had recreation almost every Sunday night. My first group of junior highs never got to go camping or canoeing, simply because I am not much at "roughing it."

4) *Youth ministry doesn't have to be the only involvement of the adult in the life of the church.* Since this approach asks for a smaller time commitment, any

of the leaders has time to work in other areas, such as the worship committee, or to head a task force, or take a leadership role in the Women of the Church. In the old system the recruited advisors had to give an entire year to youth work. They did not have time for anything else.

5) *The lower time commitment enables the adult to say "I can," "I can handle that."* One of the delights of this new approach is the positive responses I have had to recruitment. People actually say yes. What we are used to in recruiting youth leaders is mostly negative. We are usually turned down. The reason adults say yes to this approach is that they see it as a commitment they can handle. Many times folks have said: "I have always wanted to work with youth but feared I couldn't handle that big a job. Now I can say yes. This I can do." It's just not as overwhelming as it used to be.

6) *It is a great way to get new members involved.* Lyle Schaller, author of *Assimilating New Members,*[1] has said that if you don't get new members involved in some capacity within the first year of their joining, then chances are these folks will not be active members. But ask them to take charge of a youth group? Now that's asking too much! Often new members, anxious to get involved, say yes. Then after a year of being thrown to the wolves, they not only swear never to be youth advisors again, but come close to never again showing their faces at their new church home. We put new members in a dreadful position by asking them to be youth leaders. They want to be involved. But they don't want to fail or make fools of themselves.

The leadership team approach offers a solution to this problem. The new member can agree to this smaller time commitment which has a guarantee of support from other members. He or she can feel good about giving it a try. And, it is not a bad way to orient new members to participation in leadership roles. They can go on from here to other areas of involvement.

Benefits to the Church

1) *The possibility of having a successful, active youth program.* With this many folks working together, supporting each other, and with a loaded calendar of activities, chances are your church could have a strong youth program in the next couple of years. A youth ministry happens only when a lot of time and effort have been expended. To be realistic, one youth leader does not have that much time or effort. Despair, a common ailment usually noticed in January, can be eliminated by the work of a supporting team. With this

approach, for every tired leader there are two more to give a boost.

2) *You now have a reservoir of involved, trained (we hope) leaders.* If the process is carried out as prescribed, which means four sessions of training for all leaders, then you have a possible twenty-four to twenty-six folks with skills pertaining to youth ministry. After several years the number may double, allowing for a certain amount of attrition. Many of the same leaders will return to work another year. After all, they won't be overworked or burned out.

This same group of adults will have had a year of active involvement in the life of the church. If this has been a positive experience you will see them again, in other leadership roles. The community built not only between youth and adults but among team members is conducive to further participation. The picture of the church down the road will change. No longer is 10% of the membership doing 90% of the work. A new pattern is emerging—increased active participation by all ages in the life of the congregation. A hopeful sign.

3) *Recruiting leaders becomes less of a burden. And a bonus: new coordinators.* The church has a new set of adults enthusiastic about and actively working with youth ministry. Out of this group may come the next senior high coordinator and junior high coordinator. Even after one year, these adults will know enough about this new approach to be trained as coordinators. The team will also become the advocates for youth ministry. And we badly need advocates. Word will get around about the "exciting youth program." First of all, because the youth will be more visible, more active in the life of the church. And second, because the adult leaders will spread the word. As good news spreads, more adults are likely to become interested in serving on the youth ministry team.

4) *It is a great way to get new members involved.* Again, I am repeating for emphasis. As was said, it is a benefit to new members to have this kind of opportunity to volunteer for a low-time-commitment, high-support-level job. It is even more beneficial for the church. The church needs to find ways to involve new members.

5) *You are not stuck with a leader you wish you did not have.* It happens every year. Frustrated from not being able to find a youth advisor, the church ends up taking anybody it can get. And there are some people who should not be youth leaders. This is a sticky problem, especially when the good-hearted soul volunteers.

Youth Ministry: The New Team Approach

It seems so seldom that anyone volunteers for anything, that we feel it would be ungrateful to turn them down. But we need to be very careful in selecting youth leaders. Our kids are at stake.

With this new system you are not stuck with a bad choice. Or even a good choice. Even qualified folks can fail to put together a good youth program. And our kids still suffer. And it's written off as a bad year.

With so many adult leaders the youth have a variety of possible relationships. Some kids will be attracted to one of the Study leaders; another gets along better with a leader in the Service area. If one of your choices is not working out as well as you expected, you need not worry that the whole program will collapse.

Benefits to the Youth

1) *Something is happening at our church.* Too often a young person is heard to say: "We don't do anything in our youth group." It is not uncommon for a youth to ask the advisor on Sunday morning, "What are we going to do tonight?" and get the response, "You'll have to wait 'til you get there to find out." What is meant by that response is that the leader doesn't know either. A benefit of having a well-planned calendar is that the youth will know what's happening Sunday night. In fact, they will know what is being planned for several months. They can rattle off a list of activities to their friends.

This says to our youth that their church cares! The smaller churches need this well-planned program. Their youth are used to hearing all about the great things happening over at the _____ Church (the biggest church in town). Their little church has never been able to compete program-wise. Competition is not the purpose. Please, no! But seeing even the smaller churches able to provide a varied, active youth program is encouraging. Large or small, our churches need to say: "Hey kids, the church really does care about you."

2) *People do care about us.* Along the same lines, not only will the youth see that the church cares about them, but that real people care about them. It becomes obvious that somebody is going through a lot of trouble to see that youth become a part of the life of the community of faith. "There are people who want us around, who want to get to know us, who are glad we are part of the church."

3) *The youth have opportunities to know more adults.* In the old system the youth got to know Fred Brown, their leader, quite well. But he and their church school teachers were the only adults they knew. This greatly limits the growth opportunities, the possible community experiences of the youth. For too long the church has been an adult institution. Youth and their leaders were basically isolated from the rest of the church. There are many adults that youth would enjoy knowing. The church should be a place which provides a chance for significant relationships where youth are not looked upon as pupils or children, rather as people. We need to educate our congregations to treat them as such—people. If youth can get to know more adults in the church, then it is possible for youth to feel a part of their congregation.

4) *This approach offers youth a variety of adults with whom to build relationships.* In such a system we can have a great variety of personalities as leaders. Some youth will be attracted to the young, single, outgoing woman. Others may be attracted to the older, more reserved man. We need to face the fact that not all youth are attracted to "Joe College." Even though you may have heard youth say, "Our leader needs to be under thirty," in reality youth are attracted to all ages. What counts is that the adults be sincerely interested in the youth as persons, that they be accepting and treat youth as persons of worth. I have seen youth grow close to sixty-three-year-old widows, to forty-six-year-old mothers, and to thirty-two-year-old singles.

5) *Youth are exposed to a variety of leadership styles.* Once upon a time I had a clear (rather narrow) image of a youth leader. He or she was democratic in most all situations. In relation to study, it was essential that the leader be creative, non-authoritarian, one who set up learning experiences so that the students learned on their own (with little input from the leader)—which, I might add, is a good approach, but takes a well-trained teacher. I would reject "Joe College," whose approach to youth centered on his or her own engaging personality.

I have become much more open to a variety of styles since experimenting with this leadership team approach. Let me cite an example. One of my adult leaders (junior high, Fellowship category) was in charge of setting up a lock-in. He was a junior high coach, a well-liked teacher at the local junior high school. I attended the lock-in as an adult participant. I had no leadership responsibilities. This leader had capably taken care of all the details. When I arrived, he sat at a desk at the entrance to the fellowship hall, giving out materials and taking registrations. He had a whistle around his neck, which he blew whenever he wanted the attention of the group or to move on to the next activity. My first reaction was: The kids will never be comfortable with this rigidity. But, to my surprise, they were. The lock-in was fun, filled with recreation and Bible study and seen as a success by the junior highs. It was not "my style," and thus probably not the style I would recruit for leadership of a youth group. The other leaders on the team had different styles.

What I learned from this experience was that the youth could relate to varieties of style. And, that a leader could be free to establish and carry out a style which is consistent with his or her own personality. This particular leader, the coach, is one of my favorite people. I am delighted the youth can have him and hope he stays on for a few years.

This experience led me to include an exercise in the leadership training sessions on "Leadership Styles" (see chapter 16). I believe now that youth benefit from this variety and am pleased we can offer a system where varieties of styles and personalities can work together in a common task of youth ministry.

Objection

At this point, let me raise the major problem with this system, which experimenters and field testers have been working to overcome. And that is: With this many adults working with the youth at different times during the year, how do you achieve continuity in relationships between youth and adults? The same leaders will not be there every Sunday night, nor will they be on every retreat, trip, and special activity. Therefore, you could have a leader in the Service category being with the youth for a project in October and then not seeing them again until Christmas.

This is a problem that needs constant attention. The solution rests with the coordinator (see chapter 4), who needs to keep an eye on the total program. When the coordinator sees that so and so in Service is not in touch with the youth, the coordinator needs to call that leader and say: "Could you come this Sunday night just to be with the youth? No leadership responsibility, just be there to keep in touch and further relationships." The leaders know from the outset that they will be called. This informal contact with the youth is essential. Many leaders have worried over the fact that they are not getting to know the kids and have responded positively to these informal times.

One suggestion has been made that the adult leaders be invited to fellowship events—lock-ins, retreats, progressive dinners, recreation nights, eating out, bowling, skating, and to events resulting from other categories, such as mission fairs, children's parties, special events with adults in the congregation. This is a fine idea. It would be left to the discretion of the individual leadership teams, the coordinators, and the youth to decide which events would be open for invitation to all the adult leaders.

Continuity is a problem, whether it be of leadership or of youth participation. A common problem is that the same young people don't show each week. Continuity has to be worked at, with periodic evaluation by the team and the youth.

Whoever you (the reader) are, whether youth leader, director of Christian education, minister, parent, interested adult, if you like this leadership team approach and would like to see your church try it, then to a certain extent you are the one to sell it. Each chapter of this manuscript was given to three testing situations. I was asking those test churches to have someone read this chapter and explain it to ministers, to other adults, to Christian education committees and to the policy-making boards. The readers were responsible for helping me to make this concept clear.

This concept is a systematic (somewhat complicated) approach to youth ministry. You may be overwhelmed by the details in the upcoming chapters. In writing, I was anxious to offer specific guidance in setting up the youth ministry team. I tried to anticipate your questions and provide answers within the text, thus saving you from a lot of trial and error.

Trial and error, however, is inevitable, for each situation is different. Note chapter 13, which offers suggestions for adapting the process to a variety of church situations.

The next chapter deals with a theological frame of reference in which to view youth ministry. Even though the planning process (chapter 10) does not include goal setting, that is by no means to indicate that goals and purpose are unnecessary. It is essential for all who work with youth to understand and be committed to a ministry which is based upon our faith and trust in Jesus Christ. What we are doing needs to be distinctively Christian.

2
Why Youth Ministry?

A Theological Frame of Reference

A theological frame of reference—heavy words which merely mean: Why is youth ministry important? What is it that makes youth ministry distinctively Christian? What significance do our efforts with youth have in the "eternal scheme of things"? Thinking through a theological framework is necessary to keep us from having just another youth organization. It keeps us leaders centered on Jesus Christ, rather than on humanitarian or psychological principles, to guide us in our relationships to young people.

The single most important frame of reference in which to view youth ministry is the *church.* Most of this chapter will consider a biblical and theological understanding of the church. This chapter could be included in a book about any aspect of Christian education. Exploring the nature and mission of the church is essential for responsible church membership, no matter what the age of the member.

It is especially important in a book on youth ministry because the approach taken in this leadership team concept is based on the young people's participation in all aspects of the church's life. I believe young people should be taken seriously. I also believe that the church should be taken seriously. This entire book advocates high respect for young people. This chapter specifically will suggest to adult leaders that they continually wrestle with their understanding of the nature and mission of the church.

Youth Ministry Cannot Exist Apart from the Church

If you have had youth groups (junior and senior high) that have met every Sunday night for fellowship only, then I cannot consider that youth ministry. Youth ministry can happen only in the context of the church, the community of faith. The same criticism that we apply to the old argument, "I can worship God just as well on the golf course as in church," needs to be applied to youth ministry. Worship for us is more than an individual experience. Being a Christian means being a part of the community of faith, which is Christ's church. Therefore, a program in which youth have little contact with other members of the congregation and are barely aware of what goes on at their church is not youth ministry.

If youth ministry can happen only in the context of the church, then what about the many parachurch groups, such as Young Life, Campus Crusade, Fellowship of Christian Athletes, etc.? One could say that they are a part of the ministry of the church universal. However, they do not offer youth opportunities to be involved in the total life of the church. Let me say that I do affirm what these groups are doing. They fill the need of youth for what John Westerhoff calls "affiliative faith," that is, a style of faith in which "persons seek to act with others in an accepting community with a clear sense of identity."[1] Adolescents are peer-oriented and need to be where their friends are. They need to feel that they "belong." Many of these groups are meeting these needs. Large groups of youth attend Bible study and singing and grow in their faith through relationships with energetic, dedicated, paid or volunteer leaders.

Many of our churches are concerned over the success of such groups. A common response by church members is: "Look at the kids that go to Young Life. It just goes to show we need to be doing more Bible study

—and more singing!" The temptation is to copy the style of these groups because, after all, we all want a successful youth group.

Attempts at imitating such groups will not give us successful youth programs. It will only give us duplication. Those groups meet one aspect of the needs of youth in their faith development. There are many other needs to which we should be directing our energies.

So, let's applaud these groups, bless our kids who attend them, and work to expand our own youth ministry.

What Is the Church?

Since youth ministry cannot exist apart from the church, we need to examine the ministry and life of the community of faith. What is the church? What is its purpose? Whoever you are, whatever your function is in relation to youth, you yourself need to seek to understand the nature and mission of the church.

The goal for youth ministry suggested in this book could be used as a general goal for all ages in the congregation. It could be restated: That all *members* be involved in the total life of the congregation, which includes its worship, its study, its ministry within the congregation, its service, and its fellowship. Thus, youth should be given opportunities for participation in the life and mission of the church the same as all other members. Youth are members of the community of faith, the church, *now*. We must not treat them as future members.

An adequate explanation of the nature and mission of the church cannot be given in these few pages. But, since it is the church to which we look for our theological frame of reference for youth ministry, an attempt must be made here.

Biblically, we find the church defined as:
>the body of Christ,
>the family of faith,
>a royal priesthood, a holy nation, God's own
>people.

The church finds its meaning and foundation in Jesus Christ. Jesus said: "I am the vine, you are the branches. He who abides in me, and I in him, he it is that bears much fruit, for apart from me you can do nothing." (John 15:5).

> The church is founded on Jesus Christ. . . .
> We acknowledge that Christ chooses to be known in the
>   world through this community of ordinary people.
> —A Declaration of Faith[2]

> [The church is] . . . the community of those who have become involved in the cause of Jesus Christ and who witness to it as hope for all. . . .
> —Hans Küng[3]

Karl Barth, a twentieth century theologian, has referred to the church has a reality which exists because it has a commission. The commission is to proclaim God's goodness, power, and love. We who make up this community of ordinary people recognize that the goal of our existence as a community is found not in ourselves, in the goodness of our members, or in the strength of our institution, but in God and his kingdom. We are created as a community by his love, for his glory, and our destiny is his kingdom.

The commission is an exciting and challenging one. There is no exact blueprint for the church in the Bible or in theological writings. Thus, the burden and the joy of discovery and rediscovery about our relation to God, to the world, and to each other is always with us. We are called in our time and place to deny ourselves, our culture, our race, our nationality, and our economic status if need be, in order to take up the difficult and glorious struggle of knowing and doing the will of God as a community of faith.

The Community of Faith Is the Teacher of the Young

I have used the word community numerous times in this description of the nature and mission of the church. I see "community" as the central point of identification for youth. It is the youth's participation and acceptance into this community that will make the difference in a young person's faith development.

For too long we have been looking to the church school as the main vehicle by which our children, our young people, and even our adults "learn the faith." The church school has been teaching what the Bible says, what we believe, what happened in the history of the church, and what are the values for Christian living. Westerhoff, in *Will Our Children Have Faith?* has suggested that perhaps all we have as a result of this teaching is

> . . . educated atheists. For many today, Christian religion as taught in our church schools stands between them and God. . . . [We seem to think] that we have done our jobs if we teach children all *about* Christianity.
>   There is a great difference between learning about the Bible and living as a disciple of Jesus Christ. We are not saved by our knowledge, our beliefs, or our worship in the church; just as we are not saved by our actions or our religion. We are saved by the anguish and love of God, and to live according to that truth is to have faith.[4]

This should come as good news to church school teachers as well as youth advisors and leaders. You are not responsible for transmitting the faith by making sure the youth are taught the Bible, the beliefs, etc.

The church school hour is not the primary means

by which our children, youth, and adults are nurtured in the faith. I am not saying do away with Sunday morning church school (though, unfortunately, in many cases it wouldn't be missed). Rather, we need to face the fact that it is not the crucial time during which the faith is transmitted.

The main thesis of *Will Our Children Have Faith?* (a book which I highly recommend) is that it is the experience of being in the Christian community, that is, being a part of and being around all that happens within the life of the church, that nurtures our members. The community itself, the interaction between generations, is the context in which education in the faith takes place. All that happens to and with the youth "at church" has an effect on their understanding and appropriation of the Christian faith.

If youth are treated as junior members, with little respect or even concern shown for what's happening in "youth group," then the church may preach loving

and caring, but what the youth experience teaches them otherwise.

No wonder many youth think church members are hypocrites. When all youth hear are the moral implications of their behavior, what they should and should not do, they miss out on the real meaning of the Christian faith, which is the loving and freeing grace of God.

Youth also often miss out on the mission and ministry of the church. Come to think of it, a good number of adult members do too. Youth should be involved in the struggle of all Christians to respond faithfully to the call of God in Jesus Christ. This means being actively involved in worship, study, ministry in its variety of forms, service, and fellowship.

The community teaches. If youth are given opportunities to search, to question, to inquire, to evaluate right along with the rest of us, as well as opportunities to act, then they will learn what faith and faithfulness are all about. "The church is called to be a community

of corporate selves interacting with each other and the world as an expression of their commitment to the Lord of history."[5]

The Community of Faith Is a Community of Change and Challenge

Few youth today see the church as a community of change. Quite the opposite. They perceive "church" as a quiet, somewhat stuffy, stagnant place, the epitome of traditionalism. A place where the mere mention of change would make most members faint. In fact, many youth still associate "church" with the building.

What a job of reeducation we in youth ministry have! But not in the church school. At least, not there alone. We need to look continually at the quality of our ministry as congregations. Are we struggling as congregations to be faithful?

Being faithful means searching for ways to respond as the community of faith to the issues in our everyday lives and in a changing society. The challenge for the church today is to participate in the transformation of the world on the basis of the good news of Jesus Christ. This means that as a church we—children, youth, and adults—continually seek to bring good news to the poor, liberation to the oppressed, and justice and peace to all persons.

Picture youth having opportunities to participate in a community of faith that takes seriously its responsibility as the people of God to work at eliminating the injustices in our society. Imagine your youth involved in a congregation which takes action on issues relating to equality of life, prejudice, poverty, liberation, and war. This is education through the community of faith. Such experiences would contribute more to the faith development of young people than years of church school classes.

Take a look at your church, at the activities, at the kind of working and living relationships folks have with each other. What would a young person learn about the meaning of the church from the experiences he or she would have being a part of your congregation?

Youth Ministry Is Necessary

After all this talk about youth participating in the general ministry and mission of the entire church, one might think we should do away with youth ministry and replace it with intergenerational ministry. Not quite. If

Youth Ministry: The New Team Approach

we merely let youth be absorbed into the adult membership, we would run the risk of losing their interest . . . rather quickly. I would like to see youth and adults working side by side in ministry, but it takes time to develop that kind of relationship.

To move in the direction of intergenerational ministry—successfully, that is—a church needs to be engaged in meaningful specialized ministries. By that I mean it would have to have a children's ministry, a youth ministry, and perhaps several adult ministries, i.e., with singles, with the aging. Each of these groups has specific needs that require our attention before we can hope to bring about the beauty of generations living, learning, and ministering together.

Youth Have Specific Needs to Which the Church Should Be Responding

Youth should be a part of a community which is sensitive to the needs and developmental tasks of their age group. The primary developmental task of youth is identity formation—"Who am I?" and "What am I here for?" The church can play a vital role in this task because we as Christians claim our identity as children of God. Our purpose for living is given a context. We are here to discover how we can be faithful to the God who first loved us.

This almost sounds simple. All we have to do is tell youth who they are, children of God, and all will be well. Of course, it is not that easy. Youth are facing a multitude of influences which affect this identity question— their peers, parents, culture, media, school, various authority figures, and the church. Unfortunately, too many of the influences are negative. The term *teenager* seems to have a derogatory connotation. Youth have little confidence in themselves because of the put-downs they receive. This is a time when they could use a little confidence. Finding one's place in life takes confidence and perseverance. Youth need support, not criticism.

Here the church has a vital role to play. If it is true to its calling, the church can be that crucial support for young people. It can and should be the community in which youth can grow, experiment, and experience the complexities of life within the freedom and love of the Christian community. For it is this freedom and love that the youth need to make it through these years. They need the kind of love that always has a listening ear and the kind of freedom that offers the space youth need to test independence, to grow, and, especially, to make mistakes without condemnation.

This is a tall order for the church, but this love and support is basic to the nature of the community of faith. What is needed is a church which has taken seriously its ministry with youth and has committed adult leaders who can see each young person as a unique human being, created and loved by God. Members of the community of faith will need to take time to know its youth individually. The youth need this kind of respect. For they are not likely to get it elsewhere. Out of this experience of being loved and supported, our youth can discover what it means to be loved by God and to claim as their identity that they are "children of God."

Youth Need Association with Their Peers

Youth come and go and practically live in groups. It is rare to see a teenager alone. They are peer-oriented, to the point that friends become the number one influence on values and behavior. Kids like what their friends like and want what their friends want and have.

The church needs to offer both a place and a context in which youth and their friends can gather together. As important as the intergenerational experience is, the majority of youth activities happening at the church will involve just senior or junior highs as a group.

Youth ministry affirms young persons. Through youth ministry, youth meet with their peers to play, work, and learn together. They also have opportunities to minister with other age groups. This grants to youth the respect they should have. The church should be saying to youth: "We respect you now. We are not waiting for you to become adults before taking you seriously as members of the congregation."

The priority youth ministry is given in your church will make a difference in the faith and life development of the young people. The session or board which places youth work as its fourteenth priority will likely lose the opportunity to play a significant role in the young person's life. I usually can tell by looking at a church's budget just how important youth ministry is.

Youth Need Opportunities to Explore, Question, and Grow Through Various Stages of Commitment

By the time a young person has reached the beginning of the adolescent years, he or she has rather strange concepts of the Christian faith. There are a string of disconnected Bible stories, which unfortunately were most likely taught with "the moral of the story is . . ." approach.

During the junior high years, a youth can begin to put the pieces together, to see the whole picture of the Bible as the story of God's relationship to humankind. They can relate the life and teachings of Jesus to their own world, their own lives. The challenge of the church and of curriculum is to present the concepts of the Christian faith in such a way that young people can identify themselves as part of this heritage. Biblical and doctrinal concepts make sense only when youth can relate them to their present-day situations. "What does all this have to do with me?" is a central question for the searching adolescent.

The age of questioning, no matter when it occurs, is healthy and necessary for one's development. Meaningful commitment usually follows a period of questioning and searching. Unfortunately, the way most of our confirmation/commissioning classes are set up, youth make the commitment before they begin the search. Or, they make commitments before they have come to any satisfactory conclusions during their search.

When I became a communing member of the church at age twelve, it was more like graduation from the church than a beginning of responsible membership. As soon as I was confirmed, I quit church school. I can't remember if we had a youth group. If we did, I was not a part of it. They did have a nice group at the Lutheran Church, though. So I went there. I did attend Sunday services regularly with my family, but I would hardly call that responsible membership.

If we must continue the tradition of confirming youth in the younger adolescent years, let's at least add a covenantal aspect to the act of "joining." Let the youth say whether they can honestly affirm all those vows. What they cannot vow at that time, let them covenant to continue to explore, to continue to struggle with the question. At the same time, let the congregation pledge to support the youth as they grow within the faith community.[6]

Let me again emphasize the fact that youth need space. We as a church can give them that space to test their learnings. With space and loving support, youth can discover ways of responding to the call of Jesus Christ to faithfulness.

Youth Ministry Is Commitment to a Person, Jesus Christ

The last theological frame of reference in which to view youth ministry has to do with the fundamental truth of our faith, and that is, that what we are about in the church and in youth ministry is a commitment to a Person, Jesus Christ. It is in response to this commitment to Jesus Christ that we carry out our lives here on earth.

I emphasize this basic of the Christian faith to point out how commitment to a person supersedes commitment to an ideology, a belief, a cause, a theology, a value system, or even a lifestyle. You can say you are a liberationist, a humanitarian, a conservative. You can put your energies into a variety of causes—women's rights, students' rights, human welfare, civil liberty, hunger, whatever. But when the cause or belief takes precedence over a commitment to Jesus Christ, then we are in trouble. We are losing our perspective. We can get caught up and consumed by the cause. Even what I consider the most Christian of causes, the movement toward a simpler lifestyle, needs to be subordinated to a commitment to Jesus Christ.

Our values and style of life should be a result of our faithful response to Jesus Christ. We need to constantly be discovering and rediscovering who he was and is, and what that means to us today. It is a lifelong exploration.

I mention this in connection with youth ministry because youth are faced with conflicting values, causes, and ideologies. They, as we, need to learn how to assess critically these causes and ideologies in light of their faithfulness to Jesus Christ.

As leaders of youth we have many opportunities to share in this assessment. Youth and adults alike are faced with a variety of values, and thus need to support each other in the struggle to be faithful.

It seems I have come full circle. I started off with the need for youth and adults to participate together in all aspects of the life of the church, and I have concluded with youth and adults sharing together in the struggle to be faithful to Jesus Christ.

3
Getting Started

Most ideas on how to do youth ministry, or any kind of ministry, sound good on paper. But how do you turn these ideas into reality? When I introduce this concept in youth ministry workshops, it is interesting to see the responses. Advisors and ministers get excited about the concept. They talk among themselves about how this will work in their situation. But then I worry, because they often don't articulate exactly what they are going to do to get it started.

Somebody needs to list a few steps to be taken, assign responsibilities, and affix a date to the completion of the tasks. This is general planning advice that is offered in business management training as well as in church-related workshops:

—List steps to be taken.
—Assign persons to do certain tasks.
—Set date for completion of tasks.

The last element is often where strategy breaks down. Dates need to be set for completion of tasks or they will not get done.

Getting started on this venture involves this very same strategy. Whoever you are, you who have picked up this book, you will need to discover what steps need to be taken and who you need to enlist in getting this youth ministry started.

Your first job is to reread chapter 1 and go over the planning process in chapter 10. Once you feel you have a fair understanding of this approach, tell others about it. The first person you will want to talk to is whoever is responsible for youth groups in your church.

Then, mention it to the current youth advisors. Tread softly here. Some advisors will be delighted to have a structured approach to help them out. But others might take it to mean they are not doing a good job.

Talk to some youth about the new possibilities. Talk to the minister, D.C.E., youth director, parents, session or board members, and any other interested adults.

In talking with people, emphasize the benefits. Suggest to current leaders that this approach would give them a lot of support and would give them people to share in the responsibility. And it would be a way for the church to make youth ministry a high priority. Advisors often feel, and rightly so, that the church is not supporting them. They usually have to go it alone, with little help. Share these ideas as possibilities. Avoid imposing on the advisors.

Check with the powers that be on how the church should go about implementing this youth ministry approach. If you are a youth director, you probably have the authority to go ahead and start it. If you are an advisor, you will need to explain the idea to the minister, D.C.E., youth director, Christian education committee, youth task force, or whatever group is responsible for youth ministry.

The next step is to call a meeting of interested adults and youth. Current advisors and staff people should be there. You don't want to leave anyone out, for you will need all the support you can get to make this approach work.

At this meeting explain the concept. Talk about the rationale and the benefits (chapter 1). Explain the planning process described in chapter 10. You could put the schedule (page 71) on a newsprint sheet as a visual aid.

Define the steps that need to be taken to get started:

1. Recruit a coordinator.
2. Set up a calendar.
3. Recruit leaders.
4. Communicate this approach to the congregation.

Give the people time to ask questions and to express opinions and reactions.

Task Force

Appoint a task force, a small group, to be in charge of getting this concept off the ground. Have several youth on this task force. If you happen to have a youth council, they should function on this task force. This group will handle the details of the four steps.

1) Recruit a coordinator. Perhaps in talking about this concept, you found likely people to serve as coordinators. If you have a youth director, he or she could coordinate one group, and you or a current youth advisor could coordinate the other. A minister could coordinate one group. Make sure this person has a chance to read the Coordinators' Chapter, chapter 4, before making the decision.

2) Set up a calendar. Determine a date by which leaders should be recruited, dates for the orientation and training of leaders, the planning retreat, follow-up meeting, and parent/youth night.

3) Recruit leaders. Decide who will do the recruiting. It may be you, you and the coordinators, or the coordinator and current advisors. Consider all possibilities. See chapter 6 on Recruiting.

4) Communicate this approach to the congregation. The task force should brainstorm every possible way to interpret and communicate this youth ministry approach to the congregation. See chapter 12 for ideas. Decide on methods to communicate. Make assignments to get started on this interpretation and set dates for the methods to be carried out.

One of the best ways to present this idea to both the youth and the adult members is to stress the "new." This is a new approach, a new idea. Also presenting it as an experiment may have some appeal. Sometimes being a part of an experiment is an incentive to "give it your best shot." After all, unless everyone has pitched in and worked at it, there is no way to determine if the results of an experiment are successful.

The youth ministry team approach does require "working at." You will need to appeal to the youth and other church members to give this approach their support.

To involve the youth right at the start, you are asking them to buy into this expanded youth ministry program, to be willing to participate in the life of the church because the church is striving to give them more opportunities to do so. There will be many more youth activities in the coming year, some of which will involve them in an important ministry of their church —ministry to and with the congregation, ministry to the community in service, and worship, as well as fellowship and study activities.

Other Details

While in the process of setting up this new youth ministry, make sure someone on the task force is checking on other details:

1) Does the church have a policy regarding youth activities? If they do, check it out. If it is too limiting, you may need to work at getting some changes made.

2) Are there limits for structure (Sunday night only)? Can the youth have special events? lock-ins? trips? dances? plays? musicals? Any limits to recreational activities? What activities need session/board approval— such as fund raisers?

3) Do the youth eat when they meet? What kind of supper meetings are possibilities?

4) What facilities, space, and equipment are available to the youth?

5) What does the budget look like? How is the allocation for youth spent? You may be redirecting some of the funds with this new approach. And you may need to lobby for a better share than you have been allotted.

Spending a good amount of time (five or six months) setting up this approach and preparing everybody for a new thrust in youth ministry is essential to making the concept work. The first year is always rough. You may not get the youth response you expected. The second year will be better! All that you can do publicizing and interpreting ahead will make the first year a little easier. By the second year the congregation will have an idea of what is going on.

A Late Start

Suppose you are reading this book in August or September. Is it too late to start this process? Yes, maybe, and no. Yes, because you cannot possibly get the kind of support you need without the months of preparation. Maybe, because you are one fast worker if you can recruit twenty-four adults in a week! No,

because you can adapt a limited version of the leadership team approach.

Limited Versions

1) You're in a church which has had no luck recruiting advisors. It's September, and you have no advisors for senior or junior highs. You decide to go back to the folks who might have said yes if they did not have to do it every Sunday night. You present a plan in which three advisors (for each group) would use the five-category planning process, have the whole year planned out, and split up the leadership responbilities according to the activities. *Note:* This certainly is an improvement over no advisors. But, you cannot expect the level of team enthusiasm or youth response had you had time to recruit a whole team. However, you can do this limited version and start talking up the full-team approach for the following year.

2) It's September, and you have been fortunate enough to have found a couple for junior highs and a couple for senior highs. You share with them this approach. They like the planning process, for they can plan a whole year in advance. The couples decide to do the five category approach all by themselves. *Note:* You are lucky to have such ambitious adult leaders. Keep in close touch with them, for handling this balanced youth program can wear them out. Try to recruit other adults to help with specific projects during the year. Two of these committed advisors could be your coordinators for next year. Let them read this book, so they can get a good understanding of the concept.

3) You have a history of poor attendance at youth group. With senior highs you have the same single person and married couple as you did last year. But no one to work with the junior highs. So you decide to see if you can recruit ten or twelve adults to become a youth ministry team for the junior highs. You will coordinate the junior high team. You have been having enthusiastic response to the concept, so you have a good chance of running a full team next year.

In any of these limited versions, you will not likely have tremendous successes. The most important part of getting started on this venture will be starting early. If you do a lot of interpretation and keep talking up youth ministry, chances are people (youth and adults) will be enthusiastic and ready to get started.

Getting Started

4
The Coordinators' Chapter

(Job Description of Senior High and Junior High Coordinator)

Dear Coordinator: Do not be misled by the title of this chapter. All seventeen chapters of this book and the four appendices are yours to absorb. Since your job is the biggest, I find it necessary to devote a chapter to your job description. I hope this will be helpful in outlining your responsibilities. There are four basic responsibilities of the junior and senior high coordinators:

1. To work closely as a team, the two of you.
2. To know the approach, the process, and the purpose of youth ministry (chapters 1 and 2).
3. To communicate youth ministry.
4. To coordinate the leadership team.

To Work Closely as a Team

I do hope both of you coordinators like each other, for you will need to be in constant communication with each other to pull off this approach to youth ministry. In my first year of this experiment, I tried to coordinate both the junior high and senior high teams. It was next to impossible. There was a lot of confusion, and I did a sloppy job. I also tried to fill in as one of the Study leaders for both groups and have a baby in the same year. It didn't work. Had I not believed so strongly in this team approach and had very supportive leaders, this book would never have been written.

In the second year of the experiment, along came our associate minister. He coordinated senior highs and I junior highs. We did not fill in as leaders of any of the categories. Thus, our jobs were more clearly defined, the approach was ten times more successful; but, to be honest, confusion still played its part.

The responsibilities of both junior high and senior high coordinators are basically the same, even though each is running a separate youth program with a calendar full of activities. The confusion begins right at the beginning. We found out immediately the need to define whose responsibility it was to lead the orientation at the cookout and who was going to send out letters to all the leaders. Likewise, who was going to call the retreat center. (Both senior and junior highs, though they planned separately, combined for meals and recreation at the planning retreat.)

Contusion continued as we found ourselves caught not keeping up with each other's calendars. For example, both senior and junior highs eat together on Sunday nights before splitting into separate groups. The cooks usually planned to feed forty. All too often I forgot that the senior highs were having their meeting in a home, leaving only fourteen junior highs for supper. Nobody told the cook.

Another time, both groups were planning to carol at Christmas. Luckily, we realized in time that we would make a better chorus combined, and thus joined forces.

We also got sloppy about details. Which room will we meet in? The group having recreation needs the fellowship hall. The group having a film needs the darkest room. Junior highs need a large room this week for breaking into small groups. Space, equipment, newsprint. Other details, such as who will phone in information for the bulletin. Since the senior high coordinator was a minister and in the church office, I all too often assumed he would put announcements in the bulletin.

Assumptions are a danger. It is so easy to assume the other person is going to do it, to handle the details.

And there are so many details involved in coordinating youth leadership teams. Coordinators need to be willing to bother each other with phone calls. I personally am bad about phoning. If I get a busy signal I'll probably try again—next week.

Besides spending a good amount of time on the telephone, coordinators should discover their style of working together. Perhaps a once a month meeting. Or, checking with each other after youth meetings. Keep looking at your calendars. Make lists of items you need to discuss with each other.

To Know the Approach

Chapter 1 contains the basics for understanding leadership teams in youth ministry. It describes the approach and its benefits (to leaders, to youth, and to the church). Chapter 2 is an attempt to describe the why of youth ministry. We need to understand what we are doing with youth in the church. What is our purpose? What is distinctively Christian about it? What are our hopes and dreams for youth in our world today?

In chapters 3, 6, and 12, I talk about communicating this approach. You will notice that I overuse the word "enthusiasm," for the simple reason that enthusiasm is what has been lacking in youth programming. We need adults in the church who are enthusiastic about their youth and youth ministry. The coordinators definitely need to be two of these enthusiastic adults. In order to do your job, you will need to know this approach well enough to be enthusiastic about it. Reread chapters 1 and 2 and talk them over with each other.

To Communicate Youth Ministry

The coordinators need to be able to explain this approach to anybody who might be interested—to youth, prospective adult leaders, parents, session or board members, church school teachers. The biggest challenge we face in youth ministry is in trying to educate a congregation as to the purpose and the goings on in our work with young people.

Since communication is a big job for coordinators, and a year long job, I strongly suggest you get a few others who are enthusiastic about this approach. You will need help communicating. See chapters 3 and 12.

To Coordinate the Leadership Team

In order to describe the responsibilities you will have in coordinating the team, I have listed your actual "duties." The following suggestions begin with recruiting in the winter, take you through the year, and end with recruiting and planning for the following year.

1) To recruit the team. I have devoted much space in chapter 6 to a description of your responsibilities in this area, as well as guidelines for recruitment. Here again, for your sanity, it is wise to involve other adults in the recruiting process. Since you are the coordinator, one could say, "the buck stops here." You will need to organize your plan and dates for recruiting.

2) To set up the calendar for the coming year. As a

team, the two coordinators should get out a calendar and block off dates for:

—a meeting early on to elicit support for youth ministry (see chapter 3, p. 25)
—the cookout and orientation for leadership (August or September)
—the leadership training sessions
—parent and youth get-together
—cookouts for senior and junior highs
—the planning retreat (reserve a place for retreat now)
—the follow-up planning meeting
—leadership team meetings
—calendar check

These items are explained throughout the remaining chapters of this book. An index is provided, so I won't go into detail here.

Also, coordinators, check with your ministers to find out special dates in the church year, events in which youth could play an important role. Examples: mission fairs, Advent and Lenten services, stewardship, Christian Education Sunday, witness season, special offerings, special programs with invited guests.

See if you can find out dates for presbytery, district, synod, and denominational events—camps, youth conferences, rallies, leadership training. Having these dates in hand will help in your planning with the youth.

3) To call and moderate team meetings. To evaluate. Decide between you how you are going to lead the initial meetings, where both junior high and senior high teams are involved—cookouts, team meetings. I strongly suggest that both teams meet as one team in youth ministry, rather than separately. There is strength in numbers. Both teams need to feel a part of the total youth ministry task. Team members need to know each other. They can learn effectively from each other when called together as one large group. If specifics are called for—discussion of individual youth or events—the two teams can separate for a period of time during the meeting.

The two coordinators set the agenda for these meetings. A suggestion is to appoint a recorder each time. Or, decide that when one coordinator has the floor the other is writing on newsprint. Keeping a record of suggestions and decisions made by the team is crucial. Without such information, it is difficult to act on decisions made.

During the year, the two coordinators will decide when to call special meetings. Evaluation will play an important part in these meetings. Without doing some kind of evaluation, you will never know how things are

going and whether or not leaders are happy in their roles. Several areas need to be evaluated:

(a) The role of the leaders
—the support they are getting or not getting
—whether each of them feels an active part of the team
—their relation to the youth
(b) The participation of the youth
—their role as *responsible persons* (see pp. 41-42, 75)
—whether they are becoming a group
—interaction between the youth
—their participation in the life of the church
—whether they are taking leadership roles
(c) The involvement of parents
(d) Problems finding resources
(e) Interpretation of youth ministry to the congregation
—Does the congregation still not know what's going on?
(f) Problems arising from relation of coordinator to team
—lack of communiction
—Does coordinator involve team members effectively?

Plan to have an evaluation session with the youth in January and another at the end of the year. For a further look at evaluation, see chapter 5, page 45 and chapter 12, page 87.

4) To set up leadership training sessions. It is the coordinators' responsibility to set up these training sessions, but coordinators do not have to lead them. To cover areas such as age group characteristics, leader relation to youth, methods, finding and using resources, faith development of youth, you will probably need to bring in someone with skills in Christian education and youth ministry. You may be fortunate enough to have a D.C.E. or minister who has these skills.

There are suggestions for four leadership training sessions in chapter 16. Four has been an agreeable number with our leaders. We try to schedule all four within two weeks. The nights of the week are best determined by your situation. It could be Monday and Wednesday the first week, Tuesday and Thursday the second.

5) To lead the initial events with the youth and the meeting with the parents. Usually the coordinators will not be leading youth meetings on Sunday nights or any other night. However, the coordinator is probably the best choice for the very first youth meetings of a new year. If the coordinators have been working hard for the past several months (or weeks) on youth ministry, then they are the ones most aware of the need to build community within the group, to take a couple of Sunday nights for get-acquainted and group-building activities. The coordinator is also the one to introduce the youth to this new approach and to their leaders. Suggested activities for group building and getting acquainted are found in chapter 8 and in Appendix C.

A parent/youth night is suggested for the purpose of involving parents, informing them of what's happening with their kids at the church, getting their ideas, and enlisting their support. Coordinators are responsible for this night. See chapter 9 for ideas.

For all these meetings and activities, I strongly recommend that the coordinators get help from some of their leaders. A few leaders who feel comfortable with the youth could share in leading these activities. Others could help with resources and materials.

6) To set up and lead the planning retreat. The planning retreat is the most important event upon which this system is based. It is, in a sense, the climax of the leadership team's work in becoming a team whose task is youth ministry. It is the beginning of the new year for the youth. It is their initiation into planning and roles of leadership, particularly as responsible persons.

Being such an essential part of youth ministry, much energy, preparation, and effort must go into the planning retreat, primarily the effort of getting out as many youth and adult leaders as possible.

Much publicity and phoning is required. Coordinators, it is your responsibility, but get leaders to help. The details involved in getting ready for and directing the retreat are covered in chapter 10.

7) To conduct the follow-up to the planning retreat. This involves calling all youth who were not able to attend the retreat, leading a wrap-up planning meeting after the retreat, firming up details on the calendar, and making copies of the calendar for each of the youth. See chapter 11 for the specifics.

8) To coordinate publicity. For me, this is the hardest part of being a coordinator. I am just not on the ball when it comes to publicity. I have a hard time getting letters out on schedule. I procrastinate with phoning. I am bad about getting articles in the newsletter and bulletins. That is why I am anticipating all of you will have even greater successes with this approach than I have. Publicity and communication are the key to an ambitious youth ministry. Even if you do just a tiny bit better than I have at communicating, you will enjoy the rewards.

To compound my problem, I also am poor at delegating responsibility. Even when I realize my shortcomings in mailing and phoning, I don't ask someone to help me. It's amazing I've had any success at all in youth ministry. Luckily, our senior high coordinator is much better than I at communicating.

What I am saying, besides emphasizing the incredible importance of communication, is that coordinators need to encourage, sometimes push, sometimes beat each other over the head to stay ahead of the game.

There is a lot of mimeographing to be done—details of the retreat, the schedule, calendars for youth and parents, letters to parents, letters to youth. Get help in this area. More on publicity and communication in chapter 12.

9) To watch the calendar. One of the most common problems our leaders have had is keeping an eye on the calendar, knowing when their activity or study is coming up. The coordinators should be constantly watching the calendar, looking to the months ahead. Each activity needs to have an estimated date ahead on which to begin preparation. Coordinators should have on their calendars the appropriate dates to call so and so to alert that leader that his or her activity is coming up and that it is time to get the responsible persons together to begin making plans.

The coordinators need to be aware of conflicts which may come up necessitating a change in the calendar. They should check with leaders to see if they are having problems with any of the dates. Some switching can be done.

10) To oversee involvement of adult leaders. The other main problem leaders have expressed is that they did not feel they were getting to know the youth with such infrequent contact. We as coordinators had encouraged leaders to come to meetings for which they were not responsible. After a few months we realized that leaders were not taking the initiative. In evaluation, they said they would like to be there if someone would ask them specifically to come on a certain date. We did this and sure enough, they began to feel closer to the youth.

As soon as the calendar is set, the coordinators need to take note of each leader's involvement. How often does his or her category come up during the year? For example, if a Ministry Within the Congregation activity is scheduled for November and none again until March, the coordinator should call that leader, say in early December, asking if the leader would come to the next meeting. No responsibility, simply to be there with the youth. The adults respond well to opportunities to just "be" with the kids. They are not worrying about their part of the program. They can relax and enjoy the youth.

Some of the special events—Christmas caroling,

progressive dinners, projects, lock-ins, skating, carnivals, eating out, movies, parties for children—are good times to invite other leaders. These events are informal, and they usually last longer than the usual meeting. Thus, the opportunity is there for adults and youth to get to know each other better.

The leaders understand when they take on this commitment that they will be asked to come on "other" nights. Therefore, as coordinators, all you have to do is keep track of who's been around and when, and call those who have not.

11) To resource the leaders. A job that we do poorly in the church is providing resources—materials and persons—to help our teachers and leaders. There is a demand for literature in youth work. Everyone wants programmatic resources. It is so hard nowadays to know what is good without having to pay hundreds of dollars finding out.

The coordinators will have to spend time checking out resources. First, check around your own church. What is available in the area of youth ministry resources? Then check out somebody else's church, and then your district or presbytery for resource information. If you or any of your leaders have the opportunity to attend a youth ministry workshop, you should find there lists of copies of materials.

Resourcing will get complicated. The youth decide they want a mini-course on other denominations. You will need to find materials from which the Study leaders can put together a three- or four-session mini-course. Or, the junior highs want to do a children's sermon. Where do you look for help?

Chapter 17 is an annotated resource list for persons working in youth ministry. Appendix D is a detailed index to six of the best programmatic materials available, the *Strategies* and *Idealog* volumes.

People as Resources

People are valuable resources. Leaders and coordinators need to know how to use people as resources. What usually happens is the youth pick an issue or study in which they are interested—let's say careers.

The Study leader decides to get a career counselor to talk to the youth for one meeting and three persons—a lawyer, a personnel manager, and a veterinarian—to talk about their careers for another. For the third meeting, plans are made to discuss issues raised at the first and second meetings.

This is not the best way to use resource persons, for several reasons. First, the guests most likely will "talk," which is the lecture method. Lecture is not a good method with youth.

Second, it is so easy to invite someone to be a guest speaker. We rarely take the time to discuss with that person the areas we would like him or her to deal with. So, guest speakers simply "do their thing."

Third, having guest speakers inhibits planning on the part of the responsible persons. All they would do is call the guests.

How should you use resource persons? Let's carry the career illustration a bit further. (*Note:* Pass this information on to your leaders.)

The responsible persons meet with the Study leaders. Topic: careers. This planning group begins by raising questions. What do we want to know about careers? What do we want to get out of a three-session mini-course on this subject? How could certain resource people help us?

Some of the responses from the responsible persons may be: How do you find an occupation which you would really enjoy and which would not be "just a job"? How do people feel about their jobs? Have their feelings changed after working for a number of years? What problems do they encounter?

Resource persons could be of great help in this mini-course. A career counselor could deal with the first question. The three persons of different vocations could deal with the others.

Once the responsible persons decide to ask resource persons to come to youth group, they should make appointments with these people to talk over the ideas proposed by the planning group.

This is crucial. Instead of phoning people to enlist them as speakers, the Study leaders and the responsible persons should visit with the resource persons. After such a visit, the resource persons will know exactly what the group wants them to do. They will have an understanding of the purpose of the study. You would be surprised how open people are to this approach. Rather than having to give a lecture, they have a chance to participate in a carefully planned approach to their subject.

Coordinators will need to put some time and effort into this aspect of their jobs. All leaders on the team will need to learn how to use resources. Work with them. Make available the materials you have found.

12) To plan for next year. Helping the leaders, keeping track of the calendar, and evaluating as you go along will be the main jobs of the coordinators throughout the year. Which brings us to recruiting time again,

mid-winter. And it is still the coordinator's responsibility, with help.

Part of this recruiting could be the replacement of you, the coordinator. If you were not planning on coordinating the team a second year, you should have been discussing this with leaders on the team. The twenty to twenty-four leaders involved in youth ministry at your church make the best prospects for coordinators. You will need to secure coordinators no later than March in order to do a decent job of recruitment.

And so the process begins again. The first rough year is over. Hopefully, you have made notes on what to do and not to do next year. If you don't feel like you were very successful with the youth leadership team approach, don't worry. First years are tough. I am constantly cautioning youth workers not to expect much in the first year and not to give up after one year. It takes two or three years to get rolling.

Extra Tips for Coordinators

1) Keep a notebook of who you tell what. With twelve leaders, once you start making phone calls, with busy signals, no answers, and some answers, it gets very confusing by the end of the day. Did I or didn't I tell so and so. . . ? For every issue requiring communication, list the leaders and check them off when you have talked with them. Make notes of certain responses and expressed needs of individual leaders.

Noting the needs of your leaders can be of great help to you. Keep track of suggestions and who made them. Leaders will appreciate your taking their concerns and needs seriously.

2) Keep a calendar. Not just the calendar of youth activities, but one on which you note dates:

- for calling leaders to alert them of upcoming responsibilities;
- for calling those leaders who should show up just to keep in contact with the youth;
- for beginning preparation for special events, retreats, projects, etc.;
- for ordering materials;
- for sending out letters;
- for getting information into the newsletter.

One last word concerning the role of the coordinators. Should coordinators be at every gathering of the youth group? No, not every meeting. Each coordinator will need to decide just how often he or she should be there. Many coordinators will want opportunities to get to know the youth well. They will choose to be there often. It is a joy being able to attend youth group without having to worry about ''leading.'' I like to be there. I enjoy being with the kids. Sometimes I go and eat with the youth, and then stay around to talk with the cooks, who, in our situation, happen to be parents. I like having a chance to visit with the parents of our youth.

I try not to be at every gathering. If coordinators are present constantly, leaders may have a tendency to lean on them, waiting for them to make announcements or to get the meeting started. We want the individual leaders to take this responsibility.

I also worry about the youth seeing the coordinators as their advisors and all the other adults as ''aides.'' This tends to downplay the role of the leaders, which we certainly don't want to happen.

Since there is no set pattern for involvement with youth by coordinators, I recommend you do what is comfortable. An advantage of this system is that coordinators as well as team leaders are not committing themselves to an every Sunday night youth ministry. The guideline would be to attend frequently enough to know the youth and not so often as to overpower the team leaders.

5
Leaders' Chapter

If you are a leader, or are considering becoming a leader, and have read chapter 1, you now know that what you are in for is a little different from the usual youth advisor role. By using the adult leadership team approach, the church is taking a step in the direction of an ambitious and supportive youth ministry. Ambitious? Obviously. Twenty to twenty-four adults working in youth ministry. Opportunities for youth to be involved in Service, Worship, Study, Ministry Within the Congregation, Fellowship—that is, all aspects of the life of the church. Youth taking leadership roles. That's ambitious.

It is also a supportive youth ministry. You do not have to go it alone as a leader. You will not be enlisted as youth advisor and then left to sink or swim. If you have ever been a youth leader, this may have been your experience. And if that is the case, I am amazed you are still around to be reading this book.

In *The Exuberant Years* I advised leaders to go after the support they needed, whether it be bugging the minister or D.C.E. or finding a group with which they could share their needs and frustrations. In this book, I am offering a team ministry, a built-in support group, in which all members are committed to the same task.

This chapter is a job description for leaders, much

the same as the Coordinators' Chapter is the coordinators' job description. There are four sections. The first covers what it takes to be a leader, several questions for leaders to consider as they prepare to work with youth. The second and third sections deal with specific responsibilities leaders will have in their particular categories and as members of the team. In these sections I am suggesting what the church expects of its leaders.

The fourth section is crucial, for it suggests what you can expect from the church. This particular section should be shared with the Christian education committee, the session or board, the ministers, whoever represents the church. They need to know what their responsibilities are in their relation to you, the leader.

What Does It Take to Be a Leader of Youth?

How would you answer that question? "Someone under thirty who likes to go camping." That is not an unrealistic answer. There are many who would say that we need to find young adults who can do recreation. With this system we do need at least three or four for each group who do like the recreational aspects, but they don't need to be under thirty. An advantage of this approach is that we can have all ages on the team. There are masses of talented folks over thirty. Let's hope so, since that involves 60 to 85% of our congregations.

What we are looking for in youth leaders can be summed up in the following description: persons who care about youth, who like them, who are willing to be open, who are sincere and genuine. Let me pose some questions for you to consider.

1. Can You Be You?

Being you means being the person with whom you yourself are most comfortable. It means letting the kids know who you are. Be open with them. Relax. Let them know your interests, your joys, your feelings and opinions. You need not be "cool" or whatever it is you think youth want you to be. Youth know immediately when adults are trying to be something they are not, when in an effort to be liked by youth, adults act a little too much like kids. If you normally wear jeans around the house or on your off hours, go ahead and wear jeans when you are with the youth. If you never wear jeans, you will look like you are putting on a costume if you wear them to youth group. Do what is comfortable and natural for you. The youth can spot phonies.

On the other hand, leaders need not overreact by wearing a suit and tie or dress, in order to emphasize the fact that "we are the adults, and you are the kids." You need not worry about being an authority figure. Youth have plenty of authorities, at home, at school, even in the department store. The church is a place where young people can develop relationships with adults who are not caught up in being the authority figures.

Kids need adults as friends. The church provides a setting in which you can be a special friend.

2. Can You Listen?

Youth talk a lot. They long for adults who can take time to listen, without criticizing, correcting, or making moral judgments about what they have to say. Junior highs are especially open to conversations with their adult leaders. They will talk all the time. Senior highs tend to be a little more reserved, but will engage in conversation with adults they can trust, with adults they sense have a genuine interest in them. Being willing to listen communicates that you care.

3. Do You Care About These Youth? Do You Really Want to Work With Them?

Once again, I am talking about commitment. The commitment to youth ministry described in this book is characterized by caring, caring enough about your youth to want to work with them, caring enough to be there, and to listen. What this question is really asking is that you consider your motivation for being a part of this team. If you agreed to be a leader out of guilt or obligation, the investment of your time and energy will not be very satisfying. By guilt and obligation I mean did you end up saying yes because (1) you just could not say no to the church; (2) you felt you ought to do your share—perhaps the church has done a lot for you and your children, and you feel the need to do your part in appreciation; (3) you knew they were having trouble finding leaders, and since nobody else would do it . . . ?

We hope you said yes because:

—you really like kids and like working with them.

—you want to be a part of the church's ministry with youth.

—you want to know more about this age group and would like to give it a try.

If you really want to work with this age group, you will probably enjoy being a part of this team ministry.

4. How Confident Are You?

This question is not meant to scare you. It merely asks if you are aware of the talents and capabilities you have. We can be very hard on ourselves, assuming we don't have much ability or creativity. This particular approach, with the five categories, offers plenty of room for persons of all interests and abilities.

Perhaps you have some teaching skills or interest in issues concerning youth. The Study category may be where you want to be. Or you have an interest in learning more about worship and varieties of worship experiences. Then, you might want to work with youth in the Worship area. Worship is also a likely place for those who have talent in drama and music.

Have you ever done volunteer work with service agencies in your community? Perhaps you have picked up some ideas which would be helpful in the Service category. Ministry Within the Congregation attracts people who would like to find ways youth can be involved with other age groups in the congregation. If you have ever worked with children, you could be bringing skills and interests to this area. Fellowship is open for all you who have experience, interests, or abilities in a variety of recreational activities. Any backpackers?

How confident are you? is not an ego question. It merely asks you to examine, perhaps discover, the skills and interests you do have and to identify those interests you would like to explore or skills you would like to acquire in youth ministry.

5. Are You Willing to Admit Lack of Knowledge?

One of the problems we face in the church is the reluctance of people to take a leadership or teaching responsibility because they feel inadequate when it comes to biblical and theological knowledge or knowledge of the workings of the church. Along with this feeling of inadequacy is a feeling of compulsion that we must teach youth Christianity, teach them the Bible. This compulsion can be illustrated by the image of the adult teacher pouring knowledge into the bottle, youth. Unfortunately, any amount of pouring does not result in faithful Christian young people. So we have to abandon the image of adult leader with a wealth of biblical knowledge to fill young heads.

Contrary to this image, picture you, adult leader, and youth journeying together, struggling to make sense out of our complicated lives, digging into the task of a ministry of sharing God's love with each other in the community we call the church, discovering the meaning of the good news of Jesus Christ, who came not to judge, but to save, not to be served, but to serve, and who reveals to us who God is and what we can be in him. Quite a task. A lifelong task, one which none of us can accomplish by ourselves. And certainly not one which can be packaged into a bottle of information to be poured into young people.

The church is asking you leaders to be willing to join this task, to admit to young people that you don't have all the answers. Admitting that is a step towards working together on this journey.

6. Can You Be Open and Honest with the Youth?

Not only open and honest about not having the answers, but open to their ideas, again, willing to listen and consider new opinions, new ways of seeing things.

Being honest also involves being honest about your attitude towards their behavior. There will be times when you will want to praise them for the way they handle certain situations. There will be other times when their behavior will make you want to scream and turn into a strict disciplinarian. Rather than lay down the law, let them know what disturbs you, and then guide them in discovering ways to eliminate the problem.

Discipline questions are quite common among youth workers, more so among church school teachers than group leaders. For a discussion of this issue, see page 46.

There is another aspect of openness which needs consideration. Leaders need to be open to new methods and new ways of relating to youth. They need to be open to training and willing to try new approaches. One leader may never have experienced a role play and is, therefore, reluctant to try it. There are many methods, ideas, possible activities which are new to leaders. Having two leaders per category is an advantage. They can encourage each other to try new ideas.

7. Can You Be Flexible?

Being flexible means being willing to adjust your plans (or even scratch your plans) for any given activity. By keeping a keen eye on the participation of the youth and by being able to communicate with them, adult leaders will know when to make changes in plans. Having another leader in your category as well as responsible persons who have planned the activity or study is of great value. You don't have to make the decision to alter plans alone.

A frequent dilemma of youth leaders is: *To cancel or not to cancel?* Let me caution against canceling activities, especially special events. An illustration: You are planning a roller skating party. You decide to have the youth call in by Thursday if they are planning to attend. Thursday rolls around and you have four signed up. Frustrated, you cancel the party.

Experience has shown that youth (senior and junior highs alike) forget they were supposed to call in by a certain date. Many leaders firmly believe youth ought to be responsible enough to make this kind of commitment. True, they should. But my experience has been that we cancel too much because of this. I strongly feel that we need to pull out all the stops to carry through with planned activities. Which means I would suggest the leaders and responsible persons get on the phone and encourage kids to go, even though the deadline (Thursday) has arrived.

This is important for churches which have been having low turnouts and are struggling to launch a youth ministry. A reason for low participation is often that the youth are used to "not much happening at our church." It we cancel too often, the problem is compounded. Nothing will happen at our church. However, if we go all out and get eight kids at that skating party, then they can say that the church has sponsored a skating party. In January the youth can look back and see that their group has had a lot of activities. Once the youth get used to having something happen at the church, participation will increase.

For events such as retreats, we need to publicize and push and do all we can to fill the number needed to have the retreat. There is usually a fee for retreat places and food involved, so we do need to know how many are going. But to sit back and wait for youth to call in is a mistake. If you really want to have that retreat and have it be somewhat successful, you will have to actively encourage youth to go.

Responsibilities of a Leader

We have been talking about qualities of youth leaders. In this section we will get down to specifics. Just exactly what are your responsibilities? Basically four:

1. To build relationships.
2. To plan and carry out activities in your category.
3. To evaluate.
4. To involve the youth.

1. To Build Relationships

One of the best pieces of advice I ever was given about youth work had to do with the relationship leaders can cultivate with each individual young person in the church. The advice was this: If you would spend one half-hour with each of the youth, in conversation, getting to know that young person, you would accomplish more in ministry than a whole year of Sunday night programs. An entire year could go by, with fun and fellowship, and the leaders could come away feeling empty, wondering if it was worth the effort.

Building relationships is the most important part of a leader's role. Get to know the kids. This leadership team approach creates a problem in this respect. You may only see the youth seven or eight times a year, depending on the kind of activities planned in your category.

At Shelby Presbyterian Church we became aware of this problem towards the end of the first year. As coordinator, I encouraged leaders to come to youth group on nights when they were not the responsible leaders, just to be there. It was hard for leaders to take the initiative. We worked through this problem, by making it the coordinator's responsibility to oversee the involvement of all team members and to call folks periodically to come on these extra nights. We found that specials—retreats, ski trips, lock-ins, parties, progressive dinners—were good occasions to ask various leaders to join in. These are informal occasions, usually longer than the average youth meetings. Thus, leaders had time to build relationships.

So, if your coordinator keeps up with his or her responsibility, you will be asked to come to extra youth gatherings. These are fun times. You can relax, for you have no leadership responsibilities. You will have a chance to talk, recreate, worship, and/or work with the youth on these occasions.

Get to know these kids, their interests, concerns. Let them know you. *A tip:* Find out something about each of the youth that is ongoing. By that I mean something they are involved in which you can continue to discuss at different times over the months. For example:

—the young person who is on the tennis team
—the one who has just acquired a pet snake
—the one who goes backpacking and spelunking every weekend
—the one who has an unusual job, or even a dull job
—the one who is learning the latest dances
—the one who is in a play
—the one who has a brat little sister

Find something distinctive about each of the youth. It will help in getting to know them and feeling comfortable with them.

Likewise, let them know specific things about you. It is delightful when they learn something funny about

you. Back in the early '70s, my group of junior highs gave me grief about my "floods." Floods was the word they used for too short and thus ridiculous, "uncool"-looking jeans, of which I had a pair. Now they give me a hard time about wearing a bandana scarf. If I ever come to a youth gathering with just set, curly hair (my hair is unmercifully straight), I always get a resounding exclamation: "You washed your hair!" Now that I have children, they always ask me about J.B. and Lorinda. The ones who get really comfortable want to know what it's like being married to a minister.

Another part of the relationship-building responsibility is the necessity of building relationships within the group. Kids have their own group of friends and can be very rejecting to those outside their little circle. Gradually youth begin to realize that we in the church are "into" community building, the loving and caring for all persons.

Building community within your group is not easy. Much planning will be necessary to see that kids mix. I strongly recommend using arbitrary small groupings. That is, when an activity calls for breaking into smaller groups or a long trip requires riding in three cars, we leaders arbitrarily assign the youth to these smaller groups. If we left them to break into groups on their own, the same groupings would occur and not one would get to knew another person outside of their own close friends.

Group builders are a valuable method for building community within a group. In this youth ministry approach it is suggested that the first few meetings of the year be spent in group building. (See Appendix C.) Throughout the year various group-building activities are necessary for several reasons: (1) to keep the kids from falling back into their cliques; (2) to assimilate a new youth who joins the group mid-year; and (3) to help you the leader in getting to know the kids as you carry out your activities with them.

2. To Plan and Carry Out the Activities in Your Category

Your job as leader begins, in a sense, when you are recruited. At that time you will need to be thinking about your category, meeting with the other leader in your category, and talking with him or her of the possibilities. It is a relief to have a partner in this venture. Together you can come up with many more ideas than if you had to go it alone.

WORSHIP: If you are in this category, start by finding out what the youth have done in worship. What could your youth do? Is your church willing to have youth take part in Sunday morning services? Could

they do a whole service? Are they free to schedule worship at other times, i.e., after a football game or early on a school morning? Who would be your contact person in worship—minister, worship committee, session or board? Could they make banners or other special helps in worship? Would the church approve of guitars, liturgical dance? Check with other churches and youth leaders for ideas on how youth can be involved in worship.

STUDY leaders: What topics, issues, studies have the youth dealt with? What is the content of their church school curriculum? Talk with church school teachers. What methods have they found successful? How would they assess participation by the youth? What are some ideas you have for possible study topics? Look at materials, such as the *Idealog* and *Strategies* volumes (see Appendix D) for ideas on how study units can be constructed.

MINISTRY WITHIN THE CONGREGATION: Where are youth presently participating in the life of your church? Do they teach in the church school with younger grades, help with vacation Bible school? Are they on committees? What contact do they have with older members? On what occasions could youth take an active role—stewardship, mission emphasis, Advent and Lenten activities, annual special events? Brainstorm with your category partner ideas which youth might do. Talk with ministers, session or board members, D.C.E., teachers.

SERVICE: How have youth been involved in service to your local community? Any projects? Do any of your youth do volunteer work? Explore your community. What kinds of agencies operate in your town—social services? mental health? Red Cross? hospital and nursing homes? child care programs? Talk with persons in these agencies. They may be able to use youth in some aspect of their program. Explore possibilities for service. (See Appendix B.) Also check out *Idealog* and *Strategies* volumes (Appendix D).

FELLOWSHIP: Find out what the youth have done in the area of recreation, socials, fun times. What kinds of trips, retreats, lock-ins, and other special events have they had? Have they done group-building activities? How often? Talk with other leaders for ideas.

For ideas in all these categories, see Appendix B.

Your Role in the Planning Retreat. The next major responsibility is to gather these ideas you have been exploring and list them on a sheet, such as the one on the following page. This form will be used when youth and leaders first meet together at their cookout.

For the planning retreat (described in chapter 10), you will need to list on newsprint three or four ideas which the youth could possibly do in your category. At

What Has Happened	What We Would Like to See Happen
STUDY	STUDY
WORSHIP	WORSHIP
MINISTRY WITHIN CONGREGATION	MINISTRY WITHIN CONGREGATION
SERVICE (outside congregation)	SERVICE
FELLOWSHIP	FELLOWSHIP

the retreat the youth will add to this list and then choose three or four which they will do for their year's program. At one of the training sessions, you will be given newsprint and an opportunity to prepare this list for the retreat.

Make every possible effort to be at the retreat. The retreat is the kick-off event, the time when the youth will plan their entire year. A retreat setting gives you time to get to know the youth and to be comfortable being a part of this team ministry. If you have to miss the retreat, it will be harder for you to feel a part of this effort. Leaders have related that not being in on the retreat was the major cause of a slowness in becoming a part of the team. They found that they had a harder time relating to the youth. They were not as enthusiastic as other leaders about working on the leadership team.

If you absolutely cannot make the retreat, make sure to be at the follow-up meeting (described in chapter 11). The follow-up is scheduled to give those youth and leaders who were not at the retreat a chance to get on board.

The coordinators lead the retreat and may ask you to assist in various ways. You will be asked to share with the group the ideas which were suggested in your category and the three or four activities which emerged as high priority items for the year. Chapter 10 describes the process involved and your part in the retreat.

Other than this responsibility, the retreat is yours to enjoy and an opportunity for you to get to know the kids.

Keeping Up with the Calendar. After the follow-up planning meeting, coordinators will mail out the calendars. You will then know exactly when your category comes up. You will need to keep track of the calendar, looking ahead, so you will have plenty of time for preparation. Keeping an eye on the calendar is necessary in case dates and plans have to be changed.

Working with the Responsible Persons (the Planning Group). At the retreat and the follow-up meeting, youth will be asked to sign up as *responsible persons* (see chapter 10, p. 75). Find out who these kids are, for they will be the ones with whom you will plan the activities in your category. You will need to call them a month before the activity (longer for ski trips and such special events) to ask them to meet with you, say for twenty minutes after one of their meetings, to

Youth Ministry: The New Team Approach

start planning for the activity. You may find that you will need to meet one or more times to plan.

These youth will be of invaluable help to you. They are the sounding board for ideas you have. They can tell you if an idea is too childish or has been overdone. And, they themselves have excellent ideas which you never thought of.

I cannot emphasize enough the importance of responsible persons. It gives each and every young person a chance to be "in" on the planning of activities for his or her group. It gives you a chance to work individually with two or three at a time, thus, an opportunity for "building relationships."

An incident was related to me which confirms the need for responsible persons. A youth group was planning a sex education mini-course. The leader planned it alone. For one of the sessions, an obstetrician-gynecologist was invited. The leader wanted the youth to be free enough to ask him questions, but figured they might be too embarrassed to speak up. So he got the idea of having them write their questions anonymously on cards and hand them in.

At the youth meeting, the obstetrician was late (or didn't show, I'm not sure which). The leader went ahead and had the youth write out their questions. He collected them and read through several. The kids had decided to have a heyday and wrote the grossest questions they could think of. The leader became so embarrassed and angry that he not only scolded the youth, but canceled their annual spring fun trip.

What would have happened had he had a planning group of responsible persons? Let's speculate. He would have related his idea about the anonymous cards and, with a few snickers, the responsible persons would have clued him in that the kids might respond with crude questions. Alerted to this possibility, the planning group might then have scratched this idea, or they might have discussed how such questions may not embarrass the obstetrician, who could ignore certain ones and answer those he judged helpful. One nice thing about responsible persons is that they can get leaders out of jams before they get into them.

At the planning meeting with these two or three responsible persons, make sure you work through the purpose of the activity. What is it we want to happen during and because of this activity? Consider how the sequence of the exercises and activities accomplishes your purpose.

The responsible persons can take responsibilities beyond the planning. Some can purchase and gather needed materials. Others can set up the room. Others can clean up. And in some cases youth can take the leadership role. For example, if you are planning to break into small groups, the responsible persons can be the leaders in the small group, explaining the task.

Plan to get together with the responsible persons after the activity to evaluate. See suggestions for evaluation on page 45.

Your Responsibility at the Activity, Event, Project.

a) To gather the needed materials and resources. To set up the room. Responsible persons may be helping with this.

b) To be there, early, before any of the youth arrive. It is a lonely feeling being a young person sitting on the

doorstep waiting for a leader to open up.

c) To facilitate interaction within the group. Hopefully your program plans will be designed to involve all youth who are there. Be conscious of those who are being left out. Try to draw them in. Give them personal attention. Talk over this problem with your responsible persons.

d) Handling problems that may arise. If the problem is rowdy behavior and lack of participation, see page 46. I cannot guess at the number and kinds of problems which could come up. The only advice is to be flexible and try not to overreact (like the leader with the sex education course).

3. To Evaluate

It is difficult to know whether you have accomplished anything during the year or during an activity or study unless you do some kind of evaluation. Evaluation works best when it is an ongoing process, when it becomes a natural part of the youth program.

Areas for Evaluation. There are several areas that need evaluation:

(a) Your role as leader

In order to assess your role as leader, consider the following questions by yourself and with your category partner:

Do you like what you are doing with the youth? If not, why not? Could it be a lack of preparation?

Are you using the responsible persons? If not, you may not be getting helpful feedback from the youth.

Do you feel that you are not getting to know the youth well enough? (Consider attending more of the group's functions.)

Are you not getting enough support from the team, coordinator, and/or church?

What do you like about your relationship to the youth? What don't you like?

(b) The working relationship with your category partner

What do you (category partners) like best about the way you work together? This can be an opportunity to affirm each other.

What could improve your working relationship?

Are you letting one partner do all the work? Sometimes when the activity is soon approaching, one leader will go ahead and plan alone and not bother the partner. Watch for this pitfall. It is often easier to go ahead and do something yourself. For the sake of the team relationship, please bother each other.

(c) Your relationship to the leadership team

Do you feel a part of the leadership team? Why or why not? (If you were unable to attend the planning retreat, or if you had to miss team meetings, it will be an uphill struggle to feel a part of this team.

Is the coordinator calling you? If not, bug him or her, and go ahead with your responsibilities. Don't let something fall through because the coordinator got too busy or forgot to contact you soon enough.

(d) The program, methods, activities

After an event, study, project, or activity, evaluate it. See the list of questions to use in evaluating with the youth in the next section.

What methods worked well with the youth?

What needed to be done differently? Note suggestions for the next time such an activity takes place.

(e) Youth participation

Are the youth participating? Why or why not?

If attendance has fallen, it may be time for a leadership team meeting. Let the coordinator know.

Relate your reactions and evaluation of an activity to the coordinator. He or she needs to know how things are going.

(f) Youth responsibility

Are the youth taking responsibility? Are they involved as responsible persons?

The responsible persons concept takes a lot of time and effort to make it work. It is so easy for category leaders to go ahead and plan by themselves. Keep pushing to get your responsible persons to meet with you. This is most important in motivating youth to participate as well as in having a youth program which the youth themselves own.

Evaluating with the Youth. Since one of the main purposes is to have the youth own the program by motivating them to be actively involved, their evaluation is essential. By asking for their opinions of an event or study, you are showing them that you respect them and their opinions, and that they are the ones who shape their own program. It is not an adult program put on for the youth.

The following are questions to use after an event, study, or series of activities:

(a) What did you like best about what we did?

(b) What did you like least?

(c) What could we have done differently?

(d) Look at our objectives. In what ways did we accomplish them? In what ways didn't we?

Note: Youth should know the purpose of an activity or study. The responsible persons are in on the discussion of the purpose and the setting of objectives right from the beginning. Likewise, at the beginning of a study, project, or activity, or when a retreat is first discussed with the group, everybody should know why we are doing it.

(e) What might we do in the future to extend or continue this series of activities?

If it is a study or mini-course, the group may want to do more, or to take action on something suggested in the study. Mini-courses often lead to Service or Ministry Within the Congregation projects related to the study. Do the youth want to repeat this particular activity next year? Or even later this year?

These evaluation suggestions are for use with the whole youth group as well as with the responsible persons.

4. To Involve the Youth—Motivate!

The most common problem in youth ministry is getting youth to come. And how do we get them to actively participate once they are there? This question has to do with motivation. What motivates youth to be a part of their church, to take active roles? What motivates one young persons's participation and another's lack of participation?

Understanding and Meeting Needs of Youth. Motivation has a lot to do with one's needs. If we need love, we will look for persons who can love us. Understanding the needs of youth is the first step toward motivating them to actively become a part of their group and their church. The next step is relating to youth in such a way that we begin to meet those needs.

Simply stated, the needs of all young people are:

—to be loved

—to be liked

—to be important (a sense of worth)

—to be understood

—to belong

—to receive attention

—to be independent

Thus, we can motivate youth if we:

—love them

—like them, accept them

—respect them, treat them as important individuals, give them responsibility

—try to understand them, listen to them

—help them feel a part of the group and work to build an accepting community

—give them attention (individually)

—give them space, freedom to be their unique selves, freedom to make decisions

If you are conscious of each of the above in your relationship with the youth, gradually more young people will be attracted to what's going on at their church.

Other Aspects of Motivation. There are two other aspects of motivation relevant to youth ministry:

a) Youth are motivated if they see that something is happening at their church, if they see lots of activity. With this ambitious an approach the youth will have a calendar full of activities. Inactive young people may be motivated for the first time to become involved in the life of the church.

b) Youth are motivated to be involved if they have responsibility for their own program, if they have opportunities to make decisions. This approach is designed to engage youth in the decision-making process. That is why the responsible person aspect is so important. Each and every young person can be in on the planning and the carrying out of all the activities.

The more opportunities we give youth to make decisions and take responsibility, the more likely they will be motivated to actively participate. This is what is meant by ownership. The youth program is no longer an adult program to be set before the youth. It is theirs!

Much of the problem of "getting the youth to come" will be taken care of through the approach to youth ministry described in this book. Your main concern will be the first aspect of motivation discussed here—that of being aware of their needs and working to meet those needs, which is basically building relationships with the individual youth.

Discipline. A common concern among youth leaders is "discipline." How do I handle kids who are acting out or acting up? There are always one or two in a group who cause problems. Often we say, "Oh, they just want attention." Very true. And that should alert us to the fact that attention is what they need—some form of positive attention.

The youth who continually act up usually have some problems—insecurity, inability to get along with friends or parents, as well as other problems. Often these young people are not getting positive attention at home or school. What is ironic is that though their need is to be liked and loved, their actions drive people to dislike them.

As youth leaders, we need to like these kids and give them attention. Give them specific responsibilities. Look for special talents and abilities. Let them do something that gives them a sense of worth.

In certain cases, you may need to talk with the obnoxious one separately. Try to work out an agreement with him or her about the disruptive behavior.

If the disruptive behavior involves half the group, then the group itself needs to deal with it. It helps to let the youth set their own standards of behavior. They decide what is to be done about rowdiness and other problems. Then when the problem arises, there is peer pressure to conform. And you, the leader, can enforce their decisions without feeling like a "meanie." After all, they made the rules.

One benefit of this systematic approach to youth ministry is that it takes care of many of your "discipline problems." When youth are involved in planning and leadership and their activities are participant-oriented, there seem to be much fewer problems in this area. With the old method—adult leader who does all the planning and leading—the youth merely came to be, in a sense, "entertained." They had no investment in the program, no ownership. With this approach you should see "discipline problems" lessen.

One last word: Discipline is a concern of parents and school teachers. It should be at the bottom of your list of concerns. Your relationship with the youth and their involvement in the life of the church are much more important. Working toward the development of

these should keep the discipline problems down.

Your Responsibilities as a Member of the Leadership Team

I never realized this chapter would be so long. Hope you are not overwhelmed by the responsibilities of being a leader. The success of the team approach is contingent upon the commitment of each member to the team.

1. Be a Youth Advocate

You will function better as a leader if you are enthusiastic about youth ministry and are committed to it. We coordinators hope you will become an advocate for youth and youth ministry. This means talking and sharing with others what is happening with youth at the church. It means becoming aware of the situations and needs of youth in your area. It means speaking up for youth, taking their side in issues that affect them, which means troubling your church with concerns in youth ministry. Keep after the congregation and the ministers if you sense they are relegating youth to an insignificant "corner" of the life of the church.

2. Be Willing to Participate in Team Meetings

The team needs your ideas, your suggestions, your evaluation. Let the team know your needs in your specific area. That is the only way you all can function as a team.

3. Be Willing to Get Involved Right at the Start

Take advantage of the training sessions offered at

the beginning of the year. It makes for a busy September. But it will make all the difference in the world in building your confidence as a leader. Building an effective team requires "team building." That is why this approach calls for quite a bit of your time during that first month.

4. Call on Each Other for Help

Call on your coordinator. Get the help you need. Bother each other. It can become a lonely task if you don't. Coordinators and church staff get busy and may not offer the help you need. *Don't let the church let you down!*

5. Be Willing to Get to Know the Youth

Be ready to respond to the coordinator's call inviting you to "be there" for certain activities for which you are not responsible. I hope your coordinators will carry through with this responsibility of calling you.

What You Can Expect from the Church

This whole chapter has been devoted to the expectations that the church and youth ministry have of you as a leader. You have a right to expect certain things from the church In return.

1. Support

If this approach is working as it should, you have a whole team of folks supporting you. They are pulling for you. If we communicate properly to parents the church's concern for their youth, then you should have parents pulling for you. It is very rewarding to see parents expressing appreciation and saying "this is what we hoped someday would be happening at our church."

You are important in youth ministry. They really cannot do without you. You have a right to expect sup-port and encouragement from ministers, coordinators, and church members. If you are not getting the support, again I say: Bug somebody! *Don't let the church let you down!*

2. Resources

You have a right to expect the church to supply you with a variety of resources, from money, food, and retreat sites to books, materials, names of resource persons, projectors, newsprint, whatever you need. Please do not be shy in asking for these.

3. Training

The church should make available to you training sessions, workshops. In this system, four training sessions are built into the approach. Take advantage of them. The church should also let you know when presbyteries, districts, and synods are sponsoring youth ministry workshops. Ask!

4. Publicity

You should expect support for the program by the church making an effort to publicize youth activities. We in the church often do a lousy job of publicity. Make sure youth activities get written up in newsletters and announced in bulletins. Get the kids to make posters for upcoming events. You will no doubt have to keep after the church in the area of publicity.

If you are still with me and not too overwhelmed, I think I can honestly say that you are in for a good time and an exciting part of ministry. Do read the rest of this book and try to get on board in the beginning. It can be a rewarding experience working together with a group that is committed to the same task of youth ministry.

6
Recruiting

If you who are reading this chapter are responsible for recruiting, take heart—it won't be as bad as you think. Normally recruiting is a headache. All who must do it seldom look forward to it. Unfortunately this attitude is reflected in our efforts at recruitment. If you have ever done it, you have probably experienced the sick feeling of being turned down. As much as it hits us personally, we shouldn't take it personally. In an all-out effort not to be refused, we often misrepresent the job we are asking folks to do. We try to make it sound easy. "It won't take much time. And it's only for a year." We don't dare talk about serious commitment.

This chapter offers general guidelines for recruiting which can be applied to any task of enlistment, and specifics related to recruiting a youth leadership team.

Who Should Do the Recruiting?

Who should do the recruiting? Someone who knows this leadership team concept, the process and the benefits (see chapter 1), and knows it well enough to talk about it without notes. It should be someone who is enthusiastic about this approach, one who is committed to it. We want enthusiastic and committed leaders, so we need those qualities in the recruiter. Enthusiasm is infectious. Persons who are truly excited about what is happening in their church in youth ministry can convey that enthusiasm to potential leaders.

Whose responsibility is it? It may be yours, if you know the approach and are enthusiastic about it. If your church is trying this approach for the first time, the recruiter may be the coordinator, minister, D.C.E., youth division chairperson, youth leader or teacher. Once the system is underway, it is primarily the responsibility of the coordinators to recruit. They may choose to involve several of the leadership team members in the process. For example, when approaching someone

for Ministry Within the Congregation, the coordinator and the present Ministry Within the Congregation leader would make a good recruiting team.

Who Do You Recruit?

Talk with staff (ministers, D.C.E., youth director) and make a list of possible adults to consider for the leadership team.

Talk with the present and former youth advisors. They might be able to suggest persons who have helped out or shown interest in youth ministry. They can suggest parents who may have capabilities to offer the team.

Talk with the youth. Get their ideas on prospective leaders.

Basic Guidelines for Recruiting

1) *Start early.* Since you need ten to twelve people for each group (senior highs, junior highs), you would be pressed for time if you didn't start early. You don't want to rush to fill slots. Set up a decent schedule of visits, giving recruiters time enough to see lots of folks without getting fatigued.

Starting early varies. For the church in which most recruiting is done in late spring and most of the summer, start as early as possible. But, if enlistment for other tasks in the church begins in January, then that is when you should start. Even if you get a late start, try not to make it a rush job.

2) *Send out a letter.* Chapter 3 suggests having a meeting of all interested adults at which this new concept of youth ministry is explained.

As a preface to recruiting, a letter should be sent to those who attended that meeting as well as others on the list prepared by you, staff, former youth advisors, and youth.

Give a brief explanation of the leadership team approach. Announce that you will be visiting lots of people to talk with them about participating in this new youth ministry venture.

3) *Make an initial phone call.* The letter was your first communication. Then, you should call to make an appointment for a visit. That initial phone call may scare you more than the actual visit. It is during this phone call that you ask permission to "get your foot in the door."

Be honest. State what you want to talk with them about. Indicate your interest in their ideas about youth ministry. Stress that you will not ask them to say yes or no during this visit. You just want to discuss possibilities. They can always say no. And, if they do, they will still benefit from knowing first hand what is happening at their church in youth ministry.

4) *Make a personal visit.* Too much recruiting is done entirely by telephone. This is far too impersonal. If the church will not take the time for personal contact, then that church probably will not give a leader much time in support. It takes at least twenty minutes just to explain this new concept. The recruiter should give the persons visited time to talk about themselves, their interests, and their reactions to the church's program. Let them offer suggestions. Take time to share your enthusiasm.

Actual time for a visit would take from one to one and a half hours. After your first couple of visits, you will get the hang of it. You will likely be more at ease and more confident.

5) *Know the facts. Take handouts with you.* During the visit, explain the concept, the categories, the involvement of youth as responsible persons, and the responsibilities of leaders.

Mimeograph several items to take with you on the visits. Consider the following:

(a) A summary of the youth ministry team approach. This would include the rationale for the approach and a listing of the benefits, especially benefits to the adult leaders.
(b) A copy of the lists under the categories, found in Appendix B.
(c) Responsibilities of leaders (see p. 38).
(d) A schedule for the leadership team (see p. 11).

In chapter 5 I have tried to outline what the church expects of the leader and what the leader can expect from the church. It is not a one-sided deal, with the church getting all it can out of the volunteers. Leaders should expect and get support from the church.

The relationship between leaders and the church should involve mutual commitments, which we could call a "covenant." The term covenant has biblical and theological roots and is central to our heritage. From kindergarten age on, covenant, God's covenanting with his people throughout history, is a central theme in the life and nurture of our people. It is fitting then in youth ministry for us to talk in terms of covenanting—between the church community and our leaders.

6) *Be honest.* About commitment, the quality commitment of energy, enthusiasm, and caring for the youth. Be honest about the time commitment. In doing so, you can honestly say that the amount of time involved is lower than the old system of one youth advisor. But you cannot tell them exactly how much time (how many Sundays or weekends) will· be involved. That is the basic "unknown" of this approach. No one knows the answer until the planning retreat. You can give potential leaders exact dates for the cookouts, the training sessions, the planning retreat, but beyond these, exact dates are not available. You can estimate the number of Sunday nights for which they would be responsible during the year: Study, a possible 9 to 12 Sunday nights; Worship, perhaps 6; Fellowship, 6 to 8, with maybe 3 overnight Fridays and/or Saturdays; Ministry Within the Congregation, a possible 5 or 6 with extra afternoons or evenings depending on activities chosen; Service, could be 3 Sunday nights and a good bit of supervision of ongoing Saturday or after-school projects.

You are asking them to buy into an unknown in this respect, but one which will become a "known" on a specific date, that of the planning retreat.

Note: Ask potential leaders to prepare (to best of their knowledge) a list of dates when they know they will be out of town. These dates can be taken into consideration in the planning of the youth calendar. For example, one leader in Fellowship may want very much to be with the youth on a backpacking trip, and therefore would want to pick a weekend when he or she would be in town. A Study leader may be away the first Sunday of every month, but need not worry, for the other Study leader could handle that Study night.

Be honest about what category you think they might be interested in. You may be wrong, but at least you will have been honest in sharing your impressions of their talents. Everyone likes to hear good things about themselves. Let them know that folks thought they did a terrific job with vacation Bible school (a

Study prospect), or showed active concern for their local problems (a Service prospect), or were a valuable member of the session (a Ministry Within the Congregation prospect).

7) *Don't do all the talking. Listen.* I value people who are good listeners. It does a lot for one's ego. We like people who are interested in us, especially in our opinions. By the way, youth like leaders who will listen to them. In surveys of youth a common trait they list of a good leader is one who "lets me say what I feel," "listens to our opinions without putting us down."

As recruiters we need to listen. This process (complicated as it may seem) requires so much talking time that we may botch our visit if we don't give the recruitees time to talk, not only to ask questions, but just to talk—about themselves, the church, their experiences in other churches. In our mobile society a good portion of those we visit will have moved within the last four years from another town, another church. They have a lot to say about likes and dislikes. We need to give them the floor. I enjoy hearing people talk about their expectations of a church. What a variety of wants and needs!

It is a learning experience. You will pick up ideas on youth programming—what the youth did in First Church, Itaska.

The art of listening is in asking good questions, questions that cannot be answered with a simple yes or no, questions that call for an opinion, an explanation, several words on the subject.

Samples: How do you feel about. . . ?
What was your experience. . . ?
What do you think. . . ?
What kinds of. . . ?
What would you change about. . . ?
What do you like best about. . . ?
What do you like least about. . . ?
Tell me about. . . ?

Listen to yourself in conversation with people. What kinds of questions do you ask? Do they encourage the other person to talk?

8) *Convey the feeling that we are struggling on this journey together.* Developing a youth ministry can be seen as a journey, one which necessitates a team, a community of folks striving and struggling (a) to provide

opportunities for youth to grow in their faith and in their relation to the church, and (b) to contribute positively to the "development of persons," that is, to help youth in decision making, valuing, in the crucial task of finding out "who I am" and "where I am going." The challenge of youth ministry is in the setting up of a structure of activities and programming within which this task can be accomplished.

In recruiting we want to convey the enthusiasm we have for this task—and convey it in such a way that the potential leader wants to be a part of the task. The pitfall of too many volunteer jobs is that the volunteer lays back. Especially within a team, it is so easy for team members to wait for the coordinator to do all the work.

In my first year with the high school band, our director gave us a pep talk, in which he said: "A band is as good as its last chair clarinet player." My face turned red, for I was the last chair clarinet player. But it motivated me to get on the ball and work hard at doing my part in making our band an "A" band. He was an enthusiastic director who cared about each band member. The enthusiasm was contagious, and we all worked hard.

Potential leaders need to feel that every leader on the team is incredibly important in making youth ministry work. Getting them "on board" right at the start is essential. They must own the task. They need to feel that we are all in this together. They need to pack their bags and come with us on the journey.

Convey to the potential leader: *You are important!* You are valuable. You are not just doing the church a favor by taking on a leadership role in youth ministry.

9) *Watch out for the pitfalls of recruitment.* What we have been saying about getting the leader on board, helping the leader own the task and feel like we're in this together, has to do with motivation. We need to watch out for the reasons the leader might say yes. We need to be aware of his or her motivation.

All too often, whether or not it is intended, recruiting comes across as laying guilt. This is the greatest pitfall. The guilt response is apparent if you sense the person saying yes for any of the following reasons:

> "The church has done a lot for me, so I should do my share in return."

> "Other people taught and led my teenager, so I owe the church a little time." (obligation)

> "Well, I haven't done anything in the church for the last two years; guess it's my turn."

> "I feel guilty saying no to the church."

> "Nobody else will do it."

These folks will not be sharing your enthusiasm for the leadership team. They will be starting off on the wrong foot and will never fully understand the purpose of youth ministry.

10) *Don't push for commitment now.* During the visit give them plenty of opportunities to ask questions. Leave them time to think about it, to talk it over with their families. Tell them you will call them in a week, not just to get their answer, but to let them know how recruitment is coming along. In this way, you are respecting them and their interest in their church. You are helping them to feel included in what is going on at the church, regardless of the outcome of their decision.

Say it straight out: "We don't want to push you into anything." No one benefits if potential leaders feel they have been pushed into accepting.

Follow up. Do remember to call them when you said you would. If you forget, they may get the feeling you were not that serious about wanting them.

11) *Ask them for suggestions of other people to call on.* This is a good tip on recruiting. I have beat my head against the wall trying to come up with a list of names of possible leaders. It's so foolish, because the best suggestions have come from the recruiting visits.

Another reason this is a good tip is that it gives the persons you are visiting an "out." Perhaps they really are not interested. They are feeling bad because they're going to turn you down. They cannot help out. But they can. They can make suggestions. They may suggest some ideal persons you never thought of. This makes them feel good. And that's good. They have contributed to youth ministry.

For persons who have not quite decided yet, asking for suggestions of other folks takes the pressure off. After visiting for an hour, this may be a welcome relief, especially if they feel they are the target of the entire conversation.

By asking for their suggestions, you are showing that you value their contribution, their ideas on who might be good in youth ministry.

12) *The home is not the only place for the visit,* although it is probably the best. One of my favorite recruiting visits consisted of a tennis match followed by a hamburger at a local fast food chain. It gave me a chance to know the woman I was recruiting as well as have an enjoyable, unhurried afternoon. Meeting for lunch is good. Meeting at the church, usually not so good. Unfortunately, people are not the most comfortable being "interviewed" at the church. They may have a tendency to feel the pressure due to guilt or obligation. Meeting a person at his or her office is a good idea

only if the person can give you enough time for this kind of visit. If you are going to be rushed, then you'll need to make other arrangements.

To Couple or Not to Couple?

Should we recruit couples—husband and wife—to serve in the same category? This issue is raised within the old system of one or two adult advisors. Should they be a married couple? There is no one right answer. It depends on the couple, how well they work together.

This problem comes up in the church school for classes which have team teachers. Often when the team teachers are married, one partner is active and the other passive, which means it really is not team teaching. For this reason I suggest that the two persons in each category not be married, that is, to each other. If both husband and wife wish to be on the youth ministry team, they could work in different categories. The exception would be in the Fellowship category. Since we are recruiting three or four adults for Fellowship, two couples can be a good choice. Or, one couple and one other person.

Besides the problem of one active, one passive, it often happens that a couple would have to be out of town. In such a case there would be no one to take their place.

There are exceptions. At our church we have a couple working with junior highs in Ministry Within the Congregation who share leadership well. You may be able to tell from the personalities of the husband and wife whether or not they could work in the same category.

What About Recruiting Parents?

Every time I do a youth ministry workshop, the question is raised: Should parents be leaders when their own sons or daughters are members of the youth group? Once again, there is no right answer. I used to say definitely no. In the old system, if parents were the advisors the youth would have them as leaders every Sunday night. Even with the best of parent/youth relationships, this was not a good idea. In the leadership team approach, I am much more open to parents as leaders. Any parent would be only one of ten to twelve leaders.

Many have argued that parents make good leaders because they have an investment in the group. It is felt that parents of youth would be more active and involved leaders than parents of preschoolers. In some cases this is true. Another reason in favor of parents as leaders is the need to involve parents in the youth program. We greatly need the support and participation of parents in youth ministry. But we need to find a variety of ways to involve them. (See chapter 9.)

If you are considering a parent of someone in the group, make sure you talk to that young person personally. Parents may tell you their son or daughter wouldn't mind. But you will need to talk with the young person. Without being offensive, ask the parents if they would mind your asking their son or daughter. If you need to, explain that consulting with the youth on this matter is showing them a kind of respect they would probably appreciate from the church.

Youth Ministry: The New Team Approach

Section B
The Process

7
The Team Begins

The leadership team members have been recruited, we hope. Sometimes we reach August and September with a couple of vacancies. Try to avoid this. It is much easier for the adults to "get onboard" if they have been recruited before the team begins to function.

The first meeting of the team should be an informal setting. A cookout is recommended, because it provides just such a setting. It is more like a social than a meeting. It is at this occasion that leaders meet each other and are able to discuss with everyone involved various aspects of the program. The concept can be clarified. Questions can be answered.

Arrange to have the cookout at the home of one of the leaders or of one of the junior or senior highs. The coordinators should be free of cooking responsibilities.

As good Presbyterians, we always eat first and meet after. Not a bad policy. After the meal, one of the best exercises for introducing each member of the team is the *Introduction Interview* (see Appendix C, no. 1). Each person is to have paper and pencil. They are to find a partner, someone they do not know well. Partners are to find out as much as they can about each other in six minutes—job, family, birth date and place, favorite food, TV shows, likes, dislikes, hobbies, strong opinions—whatever they want to ask. They are to write this information on their papers. Obviously, they are to be interviewing each other at the same time. They should keep firing questions and jotting down information.

After all have finished, have everyone gather in a circle, so that they can see each person in the group. One at a time, they are to introduce the person they interviewed, using their notes.

The process of introducing all twenty to twenty-four adults may take a good chunk of the evening. But it usually turns out to be delightful entertainment. Taking time for the exercise allows some absorption of the in-formation, so that the leaders will actually learn something about the other team members.

This is a good introductory exercise to use with youth and leaders at the youth/leader cookout (chapter 8).

The other order of business for the evening is an introduction to the team concept in youth ministry, which should take about thirty minutes (forty-five with questions).

If you feel you have time and a receptive group, you might include a round of *Virginia Reel Conversation* (App. C, no. 25) after the Introduction Interview. The Virginia Reel Conversation is a way of encouraging people to talk with each other one-to-one. It is very effective with youth and recommended for the retreat. You may want to give the leadership team a preview.

Introducing the Process

Coordinators: Review chapter 1, which explains the rationale for this approach, as well as how it works. The leaders have heard most of this information before, so you will not want to enter into a twenty-minute sales pitch. A five-minute review may clarify what they have heard before.

Then, explain how the process of planning works. To aid in this explanation, cut a stencil and mimeograph an outline like the one on page 56, with names of your leaders in each category. Each leader should receive a copy at this point. Go over it with them.

It would be wise for coordinators also to have read over the Leaders' Chapter prior to this cookout. Leaders will undoubtedly have questions about their responsibilities.

Explain exactly what responsible persons are and do. Stress the importance of working at this aspect of the process. It is crucial, if you hope to see increased youth participation in the group and in leadership roles.

Encourage all team members to attend the training sessions, the first get-together with the youth, the parent night, and the retreat. They should do everything possible to arrange to be at that retreat.

For us coordinators, this orientation cookout has been a rewarding event. It is scary to be responsible for pulling together twenty to twenty-four people of different ages and from various backgrounds to do youth ministry. We really wonder if it is going to work. Having done our homework—that is, individual recruiting—and having a fun evening planned, we are delighted to find that we have a cracker-jack team. So far, this has been our experience.

THE PLANNING PROCESS

Goal: That all youth be involved in the total life of the congregation.

The five areas of the church's life:

	Senior High	**Junior High**
Worship	Fred Lutz, Barb Bishop	Martha Jones, Bill Crum
Study	Ann Miller, Joan Rankin	Nell Davis, Ed Knox
Ministry Within Congregation	Carol Brady, Al Perry	Bud Dash, Lee Kellerman
Service	Carl Nash, Sandy Cutler	Fran Ritz, Jan Kraft
Fellowship	Mark and Diane Evans Ed and Janet Newton	Sara and Bill Christy Ned and Karen Frank

At Youth Cookout: Youth and leaders will examine what the youth did last year and will brainstorm ideas of what they might do this year.

What has happened	What we would like to see happen

Before Retreat: Leaders prepare newsprint with a few ideas in their categories.

At Retreat:

Category leaders will man their newsprint in an area of the room.

Youth will visit all five areas, add their own ideas, discuss those suggested, and pick three or four favorites.

Come together and look at all five sheets.

Discuss priorities chosen.

Put priorities on calendar (span of eight months).

Assign responsible persons (youth) for each activity.

Evaluate. Look at the calendar. Do we have balance?

8
Meeting the Youth

What are junior and senior highs like in this present age? Are they anything like we were when we were that age? Perhaps many of you on the leadership team are a little apprehensive about working with youth. It is hard to know what these kids are like if you have never worked with them.

Characteristics of Youth

In this chapter I will touch on some characteristics of younger and older adolescents and will recommend books which go into greater detail on the physical, emotional, social, spiritual, and cognitive development of youth.

Quite often in workshops I put on newsprint the sentence stem: Senior Highs are. . . . Or: Junior Highs are. . . . It amazes me that with the combined answers of participants (some youth leaders, some potential leaders), we are able to paint a fairly accurate picture of youth today. Let me share a couple of these lists.

Senior Highs

peer-oriented	overinvolved (school activities)
afraid to respond	apathetic about social issues
cliquish	consumers
trust level of adults	intelligent/knowledgeable
in question	TV addicts
apathetic	under pressure from high
selfish	expectations
loyal in friendships	bored
lack self-confidence	faddish
vulnerable	sophisticated
want answers	enthusiastic
overload of information	prejudiced
	interesting

Junior Highs

giggly	speak what they think
flighty	impressionable
peer-oriented	prejudiced
energetic	short memories
enthusiastic	inconsiderate of each other
spontaneous	mean
inquisitive	sexually awakening
honest	unpredictable
willing to do any project	insecure
loyal	don't listen
open	irresponsible
silly	not dependable
loud	
moody	

You will notice that several characteristics on the lists apply to both senior and junior highs. None of the qualities, however, can be attributed to *all* youth that age.

If you are using this chapter in one of your training sessions (see chapter 16), discuss these characteristics. Add others that come to mind.

Each Is Individual and Unique

This is the most important fact any leader needs to know about youth. The list of characteristics does not describe all junior or senior highs. Each of the youth is unique and needs to be approached as an individual. Therefore, as leaders, you need to be ready for a variety of personalities, talents, interests, moods.

Youth Today Seem More Advanced

Are youth today like we were at that age? Yes and no. Yes, they have the same needs for love, acceptance, approval, and understanding. They are fluctuating in moods. They act like children one minute and adults the next, just like we did. They are seeking independence and trying to find out who they are and what they are doing here.

And, no, they are not like we were. For one thing, they are growing up faster. Our culture has exposed them to more at an earlier age. Television has had and will continue to have an impact on their lives. It seems elementary children are doing the things we did as junior highs. They are taking languages in elementary school. My son learned Spanish words in his four-year-old nursery school. In fact, he learned to read before attending school by watching *Sesame Street* and *The Electric Company*. Girls have slumber parties at age seven. Junior high girls are wearing make-up and going

to "luncheons." One day I picked up my very sophisticatedly dressed eighth-grade babysitter after a country club luncheon.

Physically. What strikes me as unbelievable is the incredibly fast work of evolution. In just one and a half decades, the biological functions and appearance of junior highs have so drastically changed. We used to read that the junior high age was an awkward age physically—misshaped bodies, with clinging baby fat in all the wrong places, hair that wouldn't take shape, that enemy acne. Physically, the junior high age was said to be unfair to kids, for it resulted in poor self-images, which only added to the growing pains of this stage of life.

This description of junior highs as physically awkward just doesn't seem to apply anymore. True, there are some seventh and eighth graders who have the blemishes and the not-quite-yet figures. But when I look around at seventh, eighth, and ninth graders, especially the girls, it is obvious something has changed. Many girls are well developed, with gorgeous hair and skin. How often I have mistaken an eighth grader for a senior high. Except for a couple of seventh graders, if you were to visit our youth group suppers you would have a hard time telling which ones were junior highs. In fact, the only way you could tell would be to pick out the senior highs—the ones that look like college students!

Emotionally. Though not as awkward physically as we used to think, it still holds that adolescents are at an awkward stage emotionally. Baffled parents of teenagers will confirm this fact. It is an age of emotional highs and lows. Today Beth is an ecstatic young girl and tomorrow she is down in the dumps. Boy friends, girl friends, best friends can inflict an enormous amount of pain. Leaders need to be aware that these hurts are very real, that it takes a few years to be able to stabilize the joys and sorrows of everyday life.

Mentally. You may have heard it said that youth are smarter nowadays. It may not be that they are smarter (IQ-wise) but they are exposed to more and thus have much more to cope with, much more to sort through in this business of identity establishing and decision making.

One of the major differences between the younger and the older adolescent concerns their ability to sort through all that affects them, all that they are learning and experiencing. Both junior and senior highs are able to think abstractly, to consider several angles to a problem, and to understand concepts, such as faith, justice, economy. However, senior highs have more experience in this area, by virtue of having a few more years' practice. Junior highs lack this experience in judgment.

The implication of all this for leaders is that senior highs may have more rational, more complex responses to problems they encounter in their studies and in their personal lives. With junior highs, do not be surprised if in the middle of a discussion you realize nobody has any idea what you are talking about.

Idealism

One of the qualities of youth that I enjoy is their idealism. I have noticed this more with junior than senior highs. It is a quality I wish I could bottle for these kids to be put in their medicine chests for future use. They come up with such simple answers to war, economic problems, marriage problems—answers that seem to make sense. "Why doesn't somebody just go over and tell those guys in the Middle East how much happier everyone would be if they had a peace agreement?" These kids are capable of understanding the kind of love Jesus had for folks, even for "bad" people. Giving them opportunities to express their idealistic opinions can have a positive effect upon their understanding of their faith and of their lives in the years ahead.

Prejudice

At the same age (adolescence) in which we see this idealism, we also see a cold prejudice, which will often shock leaders. Prejudice toward those of other races, toward those of other economic and social levels, even toward those of other religious denominations. Much of this prejudice comes from parents, some from peers (which may also have come from parents of those peers). But it is there, and it reveals a hardness in these kids. Much is manifested in the form of poking fun.

Sexually Active

Statistics are showing that young people are sexually active at an even younger age today, and that a higher percentage of youth are engaging in sex. So, it is now possible that the "nice" girls who didn't now do. The wild bunch did. The church kids didn't. Not nowadays. The implication for the church and youth leaders is that we need to help youth sort through competing values that face them, so that they can make crucial decisions on their own.

For more in-depth reading on characteristics of youth, see:

1. *Presbyterian Youth Ministries: Youth Manual,* compiled by Jill Senior, edited by William R. Forbes (PCUS, 1979), $5.00.

   Includes sections on physical growth; sexual development; identity formation; social relationships; interests and attitudes; self, home, and community; cognitive development; and adolescents in relation to adults. Also, specific differences year by year.

2. *Creative Youth Leadership,* by Jan Corbett (Judson Press, 1977), $3.95.

   Two chapters: Myths About Youth
   Common Characteristics of Youth

3. *Young Girls: A Portrait of Adolescence,* by Gisela Konopka (Englewood Cliffs, NJ: Prentice-Hall, 1976), $2.95 pb ($3.25 in Canada).

Though written about girls, this excellent study, a result of hundreds of interviews, offers unique insights into the values, feelings, and thoughts of today's youth in regard to family, school, life goals, loneliness, drugs and alcohol, sexuality, and political-social concerns.

4. *Adolescent Development and the Life Tasks,* by Guy J. Manaster (Boston: Allyn & Bacon, 1977), $15.95.

An extensive exploration of all aspects of adolescent development—physiological, cognitive, moral, sex-role, personality. This large and expensive volume is not recommended for every leader. Rather, it is for those who are looking for the best in-depth study of adolescence.

The Cookouts

For some of you, the cookout (or some form of dinner and fun night) will be your first meeting with the youth. You should plan on having one for senior highs and their leaders, and one for junior highs and their leaders. This should be an informal gathering, at which youth and leaders can begin to get to know each other. A cookout offers the kind of informality needed and takes advantages of good weather.

Find someone to host this cookout. A parent of one of the youth would be a good choice. Coordinators and leaders should be free from food responsibilities, so that they can mingle with the kids.

We usually eat first, unless someone didn't start the charcoal early enough. Then we get out the volleyball equipment. You might plan on setting up volleyball if the host has adequate space.

After the meal, plan on using group-building activities with adults and youth together. Choose from those in Appendix C. Add your own.

The following is a possible format for group builders:

1. *Introduction Interview* (Appendix C, no. 1)

2. *Open-Ended Statements* (no. 23)
   Form small groups of four. The following are suggestions:

   (a) A TV commercial I can't stand is . . .
   (b) My favorite way to spend a Saturday is . . .
   (c) I get angry when . . .
   (d) An animal that best describes me is . . .

3. *Four Facts/One Lie* (no. 20)
   Either keep the same small groups or switch around and form new groups of four. Consider using the following:

   (a) Favorite TV show
   (b) One of the most foolish things I ever did

   (c) Something I got away with when I was a little kid
   (d) Foreign country I would like to visit

After the group builders, the coordinators should introduce the leaders and their respective categories. They should explain the five categories and the purpose of this balanced program concept. Put in a plug for the retreat—date, time, and an explanation that this is the opportunity for the youth to design their program, to choose the activities for the coming year.

Divide into small groups of four (or stay in groups from the last group-building activity). Pass out the form found on page 41. (This will need to be mimeographed ahead.) Ask the group to think back over the activities they did last year. They are to write down each activity under its appropriate category. Some, like retreats, will go under more than one. They are to write only in the left column at this point.

When most have finished, the coordinators should make a composite list on newsprint for everybody to see. Start with Worship, then Study, etc.

Looking over the entire list, ask, "In which category did we do the most?" And, "In which areas did we not do very much?" Let the youth talk about activities they liked and didn't like.

Emphasize the need for balance in the coming year and suggest that they brainstorm in their small groups every possible idea (no matter how fantastic) which they could do this coming year. Explain that you will not go over these ideas at this meeting. But you will use these ideas at the planning retreat.

Note: If there is time and the youth seem enthusiastic about their new ideas, go ahead and let them share them.

Encourage everyone to plan on being at the retreat and to get other kids from the church to go.

Put in a plug for the parent night. No doubt publicity has already gone out for this. Ask for a couple of volunteers to work with the coordinators on the activities for parent night. Wherever possible, involve youth in planning.

To close out the evening, you might have recreation, possibly the kind where those who want to leave can do so. Informal times after a gathering are good for building relationships with the new leaders. Often the kids who hang around are those who need or want to have adult leaders as friends.

9
Involving Parents

About a decade ago parents were doing everything they could to get their kids to go to youth group. It was a tough situation. The kids were made to go, and there wasn't much happening when they got there.

Now that churches have made some progress in updating youth ministry, we are hearing parents say: "Don is involved in so much. Church is just one more thing. And Sundays are our only family time."

We find parents unwilling to drive their kids to church activities. There ae so many school and sports activities requiring delivery and pickup of youth that parents don't want to make that extra trip.

We have also found several cases of parents grounding their youth from church activities as punishment. This is what strikes me as ironic. The parents have complained that the church has not offered anything for their kids. Then we start offering a really active program. The kids begin to come. They like coming. Church now qualifies as "enjoyment," and therefore is on the list of "grounding."

The church is in competition with so many activities in which kids are involved these days. More than ever, we need the parents' support. We need them on our side, not working against us.

The job facing us coordinators and leaders is how to involve parents in youth ministry and how to communicate and interpret what their youth are doing.

This is one of the issues that the task force (chapter 3) should be discussing. It should also be on the agenda of the leadership training session (chapter 16). These groups should brainstorm as many ways as they can think of to involve parents in youth ministry.

Here are ideas from one brainstorming session:

Host/hostess—having youth in their homes
Preparing meals at church
Driving

Carpooling
A parent support-group (meets monthly)
Sign-up sheet for parents—for a variety of needs which may arise during the year
Survey to identify the gifts and talents of parents
A few parents on the leadership team
Parent/youth retreat
Parent/youth dialogue
Parent/youth sports—volleyball, bowling teams, softball
Parent/youth fun night—games, fun exercises
Restaurant for parents
"Parent Roasts" (similar to television's celebrity roasts)
Parents involved in renovating the youth center or part of the building
Parent Night
—to share in dreams of what youth ministry will look like
—to see the calendar

The next step is to take action. Decide which of the ideas you will undertake. And do it!

Parent Night

Something needs to be done right at the beginning —late August, September, or October. There are two logical Parent Night possibilities. One is before the planning retreat, the other after. The first introduces parents to the five-category process and involves them with the youth in the dreaming and brainstorming of ideas in each category.

The Parent Night after the planning retreat provides an opportunity for parents to see the work that the youth have done in planning their year. They will see the names of the youth as responsible persons. They will have the calendar explained. Thus, parents will see that the church really is doing something for their youth. This meeting is a time to emphasize the necessity of their support.

I cannot say which time for the Parent Night is better. There are advantages to each. You might try one before the retreat one year and after the retreat the next. The variety is beneficial. You would not want to do the exact same Parent Night year after year.

Following are samples of two Parent Night structures. They are merely suggestions. Take what is useful to your situation and design your own. These objectives may help:

1. To give parents an introduction to youth ministry via the five-category, balanced program concept. To let them see just how many opportunities there are for youth to be involved in the church.
2. To give parents the opportunity to meet the leadership team.
3. To have a fun time—kids and parents together.
4. To enlist the participation and support of parents.

Parent Night Before the Retreat

A Parent Night held before the retreat can give parents the opportunity to be involved on the ground floor, before plans are made. In this setting parents can join in the brainstorming of ideas for activities in the five categories. Thus you are saying to parents: "We would like to hear from you. What are some of your ideas as to what might happen in youth ministry in our church?"

This schedule requires about one and a half hours. It could follow a meal or precede refreshments. An advantage of refreshments at the end of a meeting is that folks usually stay around and talk with each other.

Junior and senior highs and their parents could meet together for the meal and a "total group" game. Then they would go to two different rooms for the rest of the evening.

Or, the junior high Parent Night could be totally separate from the senior high.

Begin with a total group fun game, such as the "Coin Game" (Appendix C, no. 33), or "Stand on Numbers" (no. 29)—a favorite of junior and senior highs—or "How Many of You. . . ?" (no. 31), or "More Hamburger than Steak" (no. 30).

Figure out some way to break into well-mixed small groups, that is, groups of five, six, or seven, which have a fairly equal number of adults and kids. Numbered name tags made in advance is one way to divide. Or

see numbers 26, 27, and 28 in Appendix C.

Coordinators: After they are in their groups, you will no doubt need to rearrange some folks to keep a good ratio of adults to youth. There are usually more adults than youth at Parent Night, so your small groups may be four adults to two youth. Four to three would be a better ratio.

These small groups will stay together for the rest of the evening.

Spend twenty to thirty minutes doing three small group activities. Possibilities are numbers 18, 20, 21, 22, 23, and 24 in Appendix C.

During the last small group activity, the coordinator would pass out the mimeographed idea sheets (see p. 41).

Explain youth ministry. After all groups have finished the last activity, the coordinator should explain what the church is doing in youth ministry.

Coordinators: Review what you said at the leadership orientation.

Make this a fairly short explanation. You need not go into the rationale or the list of benefits of this approach. Consider the following points:

1. The church cares enough about the youth to see that they have opportunities to be involved in the life of the church.

2. Youth group is not just study and fellowship, but it is a ministry. (Here you can explain the five categories.)

3. The youth will take responsibility for their activities by being involved in planning and by serving as responsible persons. (Explain responsible persons.)

4. The youth need to know more adults in the congregation, and vice versa. Thus, the many leaders on the team.

5. Parents can provide a major support to this ministry by their involvement and by supporting their kids' participation.

6. Introduce the leadership team. Each leader should stand and be seen.

At this time, ask the small groups to list on the left side of the form activities the youth have done in the

Youth Ministry: The New Team Approach

last year in each of the categories. The youth will no doubt contribute the most in this exercise.

After about ten minutes, ask the small groups to brainstorm ideas in each of the five categories that the youth might do in the coming year (the right side of the form). Tell everybody that we are interested in the parents' ideas and want to allow their input in the process.

These ideas will help the category leaders and the youth at the planning retreat, where they will actually nail down activities, projects, and events for the year.

Let them work at this for fifteen minutes.

For the last five minutes, ask that one person in each group write down all the ideas that are suggested in response to the following questions:

In what ways might parents be of help and support to this youth ministry?

Thank the parents for coming, for their enthusiasm (be optimistic), and for their help.

Collect all the sheets. Make sure you have parent-involvement suggestions from each small group.

Have fun compiling this information. It should be valuable.

Make a composite list under each category and give it to the appropriate leaders. Keep the parent-involvement suggestions for the leadership team to consider, and for the youth to consider (most likely at the follow-up meeting to the planning retreat).

Parent Night After the Retreat

If you choose to have the Parent Night after the retreat, you should do it soon after. The Sunday night after the follow-up meeting is ideal. At this meeting you are saying to parents: "We have got a great year planned, and we want you to know about it. We need your help in supporting youth ministry."

This schedule also requires an hour and a half and could follow a meal or precede refreshments.

Again, junior and senior highs can meet for the meal and total group games, or you could have separate Parent Nights.

Coordinators: In preparation, have copies of the calendar (the one you will have sent to the youth—see pp. 12 and 82) available to distribute to the parents. In

this way you save on postage and eliminate more than one mailing per house.

Like the schedule for the ''before'' meeting, begin with total group games (see Appendix C). You have more time and can do two or three, since you will not be filling out idea sheets. You might do the ''Coin Game'' (no. 33), ''Stand on Numbers'' (no. 29) and ''How Many of You. . .?'' (no. 31), or ''More Hamburger than Steak'' (no. 30).

After the games, explain youth ministry. See page 64 for the main points to cover.

If junior and senior highs are joining forces for this Parent Night, you have a choice. One coordinator could explain youth ministry to the whole crowd, or you could go to separate rooms after the group games. Then each coordinator would speak to his or her own group.

The next activity is the explanation of the calendars. If you are meeting together, you would separate for this. It is a good opportunity for two or three of the youth to take leadership roles. Each would explain a portion of the calendar. Have the large posterboard calendars on the wall. Copies of the calendar can be distributed prior to the explanation.

After the explanation, coordinators should put in a plug for parent support and involvement. You could do a brainstorming session, as suggested on page 65. Or perhaps you have specific areas in which you need parent help. Go ahead and enlist their help at this meeting.

For example: You need parents to help with the meals. Ask who would be willing to help. Write their names on newsprint. Occasionally you will need drivers. Who can drive? Write down their names. Hosts and hostesses, that is, homes which would be available for occasional meetings. Get their names down.

Taking time to get the names for these responsibilities on the spot works better than passing around a sheet, or having folks sign up as they leave.

Thank them for their participation and support.

If you happen to decide to have a two-and-a-half- to three-hour event with parents, consider doing some recreation and other group-building activities which require more time. ''Sign My Card'' (no. 11) or ''Who Am I?'' (no. 10) are great openers. Consider setting up a Virginia Reel Conversation (no. 25).

A Parent Night, either before or after the retreat, will not be enough to sustain parent support throughout the year.

Coordinators and leaders: Work on ideas for involving parents throughout the year. Keep in touch with them. Periodically ask for their ideas on how parents can better support youth ministry.

Have other parent/youth events—fun nights, sports events, studies or projects.

You might ask the youth at the planning retreat to schedule into their calendars one or two more activities with parents.

So many factors contribute to the success of youth ministry. And parent support is one of them. Do work at it.

10
The Planning Retreat

The planning retreat could be considered the most important event of the year in youth ministry, both for leaders and youth. The youth may not consider it the most exciting, but it should be a highlight. It is the kickoff event, the time when the youth make their plans for the entire year. It is the first overnight gathering, with plenty of time for getting acquainted and group building. It takes time for youth and leaders to feel comfortable with each other. It also takes time to build community within the group. A retreat setting offers this kind of time.

In the youth meetings preceding the retreat, the youth have been receiving publicity as well as encouraging everybody to come. For a month the group has been mobilized to get ready for this event. This is their retreat, their time to make plans for the activities of the group. They know that their ideas are needed and that they will be the decision-makers as to the direction their group will take.

This is the event toward which the adult leadership team has been working. The category leaders have been exploring ideas. The training sessions have offered suggestions on ways to relate to youth. And now is the time to begin working as a team with the youth.

I highly recommend doing this planning at a retreat, rather than at an extended meeting. In *The Exuberant Years,* the suggested time length for the planning meeting was three hours (including supper). It can be done, but it is one rush job. By the end of the three hours, no one can remember what went on the calendar or who signed up for what as responsible persons. Even though planning can be fun (the youth usually enjoy the process of planning), there is little time for anything else in a three-hour meeting.

If, for whatever reasons, you absolutely cannot get 50% of your youth (that is, 50% of your active group)

and 50% of your leadership team to go on a retreat, then you may have to have a one-day retreat—all day Saturday, or Sunday afternoon and evening. Be sure to make this at least a seven-hour event, so that you will have time for group-building activities and a little recreation. Plan either two meals, or a snack and a meal. Meals are good times for adults and youth to chat.

Getting Ready for the Planning Retreat

Leaders: Your main preparation for the retreat will take place at one of the leadership training sessions. The coordinators will explain your responsibilities, give you a retreat schedule, and give you an opportunity to list on newsprint three or four ideas in your category (see chapter 5, p. 42). You will also have a chance to go over ideas suggested by the youth at the cookout for leaders and youth (see chapter 8) and those ideas suggested by parents and youth at the parent/youth meeting (see chapter 9).

It is basically the coordinators' responsibility to get you ready for the retreat. Therefore, from this point on, this chapter is written directly to the coordinators. You leaders may want to read through it to get an idea of exactly what is going to happen at the retreat.

Coordinators: It would be helpful to you in the planning of this retreat to ask two or three young people to meet with you. Share with them the purpose of this retreat, which is twofold: (1) becoming a group; and (2) planning. With this purpose in mind, work out a possible schedule, using the ones on pages 76-77 as examples. There are choices for group-building activities and recreation, some of which can be found in Appendix C. Check out other resources suggested in chapter 17. The youth can help in the decision making.

The only items of preparation which need to be

handled way in advance are: (1) The procurement of a retreat setting. In order to get the place you want when you want it, it is wise to reserve at least six months before the retreat date. You may want to get into a pattern, if you like the place, of setting the date and reserving the site a year in advance. (2) Food arrangements. A month of two ahead make whatever arrangements you will need. You may recruit a "cook." Or, several folks in the congregation can contribute items for each meal. One time we had two women who prepared and froze spaghetti casseroles, two made salads, three made brownie-type desserts. We bought cold cuts, cheese, and bread for one lunch, and cereal, milk, orange juice, and donuts for breakfast.

Your leaders should not be cooks. They have enough responsibilities and should be with the youth. Parents can be very helpful in food preparation. Delegate responsibility for the shopping and collection of food.

Note: This year we found that our youth happen to enjoy cooking. At the beginning of the retreat we had a sign-up sheet. Five or six kids signed up to cook, and five more to clean up after each meal.

A Week Before the Retreat

At the cookout for leaders and youth the youth filled out the idea sheets (see pp. 41, 61), on which they listed activities, studies, and events that occurred last year. And they dreamed a little—listing ideas and options in the five areas of the church's ministry, activities which the group might do in the coming year.

As coordinator, you will have a few responsibilities between this cookout and the planning meeting.

1) Compile a list of all the ideas from the idea sheets. Check over each sheet filled out by the young people. Make a composite list for each category. The list should include both "things done last year" and "ideas for this year."

Example:

Ministry Within the Congregation

Things done last year	Ideas for this year
Christmas caroling.	Christmas caroling.
Help with the nursery.	Lead fun night at fellowship dinner.
Help decorate and serve at fund-raising dinner.	Halloween party for children of our church.
	Youth write articles in church newsletter.
	Family cookout.
	Sports with adult/youth teams.

Check for duplication. Each leader needs a copy of the ideas under his or her category. The individual leaders will then add these alternatives (from the youth) to their own ideas.

During the week, the leaders should check out details on some of the ideas. For example, under Ministry Within the Congregation, one of the youth might have suggested a family camp (one or two overnights). The leader would need to call the minister or someone who could tell whether or not this idea is a possibility. The minister might also know of camp facilities available for church use.

By checking on details, the leaders will become more familiar with their areas and gain a better understanding of what youth actually can do to be active in the life of the church.

The leaders will need to put several items from the combined list of alternatives on a newsprint sheet or posterboard (with felt pen), for use at the planning meeting. This may be done at the last leadership training session.

2) Check with the leaders concerning their alternatives. What questions do they have? Any problems? If you have not done so by now, send the leaders copies of the schedule for the planning retreat, explaining what will happen, where the leaders will be taking an active role (see pp. 76-77).

3) Divide the list of youth among the leaders. Have each leader call those on his or her list to secure definite reservations for the retreat.

It is interesting to note the various reactions of leaders as they become involved in the leadership team. Some will be phoning you with ideas and spending a lot of time checking on possibilities. Others, still unsure of the whole process, will not even get the list of alternatives on newsprint. There can be a lot of misunderstandings, so check with each leader and explain clearly what they are to do to get ready for the planning retreat. Again, they are to:

(a) Combine their ideas with the youth's.
(b) Check out feasibility and details on some ideas.
(c) Reproduce the list of three or four ideas on newsprint.
(d) Phone their list of youth.
(e) Show up at the planning retreat.

4) Check on details for the retreat.
a) Check the schedule. List materials you will need —newsprint, felt pens, tape, chairs, pens and pencils, paper, recreation equipment, worship resources. Arrange with one or two leaders and/or youth to set up rooms for the different activities—group building, plan-

ning, worship. Make sure heat or air conditioning will be turned on.

b) Check on food arrangements. Give cooks and buyers an estimate of the number of participants.

c) Make sure transportation is arranged. Know who is driving. Parents often ask.

5) *Prepare for the planning process.* The actual planning should take place in a three- to three-and-a-half-hour time block after the group has had group building, some recreation, and a meal. The youth and leaders alike need time to unwind and to feel comfortable with each other in a retreat setting. A meal, recreation, and group building are the main ice breakers necessary as a preliminary to the planning.

Note the sample schedule on page 71. It is suggested that name tags be made at the beginning of the planning time. This may seem an odd time, for name tags are usually made on arrival at a meeting. However, any time is a good time to concentrate on people's names and their interests or characteristics. Also, in this case, we need the color scheme of the name tags for breaking into small groups.

Feel free to use a different name tag exercise (see nos. 3, 5, 6 in Appendix C). By all means, find a variety of group-building exercises and games from which to create your own retreat schedule. One creative woman in one of my classes used an interesting method for dividing her youth into small groups. At the beginning of one meeting, she gave each young person one of the miniature Hershey chocolate bars. Then, at the time for breaking into groups, she announced: ''All Krackels go to that corner, all Mr. Goodbars over here . . .'' and so on. She might have had two extra groups: ''All those with melted mess, over there, and those who have already eaten theirs, over here.''

For the planning part of the retreat you will need:

> lots of paper and pencils or pens
> newsprint
> tape (masking tape or package sealing tape)
> construction paper for name tags
> yarn or straight pins for name tags
> scissors (in case you did not get the yarn cut)
> felt pens
> goal statement on newsprint
> idea sheets (in case anyone needs them for
> reference, see p. 61)
> calendar—two posterboards covered with kitchen
> wrap, acetate sheets, or self-adhesive
> transparent shelf paper

Give yourself some time to prepare, for you will need to do the following:

a) Gather materials for the name tags. Tear 8'' x 11'' sheets of construction paper in half, and you will have a good size for the name tag (5½'' x 8''). You will need five colors of construction paper, for you will be assigning persons to small groups according to the colors: ''All reds go to this corner; blues, here;'' etc. Arrange the construction paper in sets of colors: one red, one blue, one yellow, one pink, one orange, then repeat. Number each name tag on the back: 1 through 20, 30, or however many you expect to attend. You will be handing them out at the beginning of the planning process. Pass them out in order; then you will have approximately the same number of persons per small group.

Cut yarn in strips long enough to tie the name tag around a person's neck; or you can use straight pins.

b) On a sheet of newsprint write the goal of youth ministry, the purpose of the youth group. Your goal should be somewhat similar to the following:

> Our goal is to be involved in the total life of our church and its ministry. The life of our church can be divided into the following categories:
>
> *Worship*   *Ministry Within the Congregation*
> *Study*   *Service (to the community)*
> *Fellowship*

c) Make a calendar of the year out of two poster-boards. One posterboard can be divided nicely into four months. Your calendar may look like:

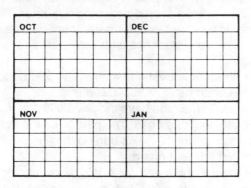

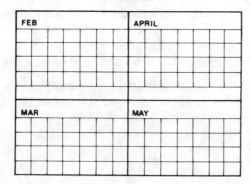

Spread a couple of sheets of acetate or self-adhesive transparent shelf paper across the face of the poster-board calendar. Or you can use plastic kitchen wrap and tape. Plan on taking a couple of hours to make the calendar.

Place on the calendar any special events from your church's calendar—congregation-wide events, such as a mission fair, special dinners, special worship services, picnics, etc. Also, find out the dates of district or area youth events. Hopefully you were able to get in touch with someone in your state or area who could give you information on larger youth events. Don't forget to check out city-wide interchurch events. And take along a school (or schools) calendar.

Room Arrangement

You will need a fairly large room with lots of open space, so that five groups can meet in one room. If that is impossible, arrange for two groups to meet in the hall, porch, or other small rooms. The small groups should be near each other.

Locate wall space where you can display all five newsprint sheets in view of the entire group.

If there are tables in the room, get them out of the way, perhaps by pushing them back against the walls

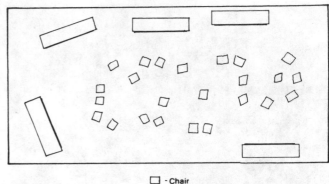

☐ - Chair

and corners. They can be used in the small groups.

There should be chairs for everyone. They do not have to be in any particular formation for the beginning of the planning. They can be scattered throughout the room. The youth will move their own chairs with the changing of activities.

The Planning Process

A sample schedule for the planning:

7:30 — Make name tags.
7:50 — Virginia Reel Conversation.
8:05 — Introduce planning process.
Introduce leaders.
8:15 — Split into small groups
and begin work on alternatives.
9:15 — Break.
9:30 — Work on options and calendar.
10:15 — Assign responsible persons.

Be flexible with the time slots. Some segments may take longer than the allotted time. Feel free to change the time structure. Be aware of the energy level. If the youth are getting tired of working on the calendar, you may want to break for twenty minutes of group recreation. Not free time—you had that at break. Rather, use games that keep them together as a group but offer a change of pace.

1) Make name tags. Give each of the youth a piece of construction paper from your prearranged numbered pile and a pen or crayon. Explain that they are to think of four or five things—interests they have, activities they like to do, hobbies, or characteristics—something that would tell us a little about themselves. They are to think of a symbol for each of these and draw it on their name tags. Once they finish, have them poke holes in the top of the name tags and tie them around their necks with pieces of yarn (or pin them on).

When they finish, they are to walk around the room, reading name tags, asking each other questions, and explaining symbols.

2) *Virginia Reel Conversation* (App. C, no. 25). When everyone has finished making name tags and has had a chance to mill around, have them each take a chair and form two lines of equal length, facing each other. Each person should be facing a partner. The two lines should be very close, for participants will be carrying on quick conversations with their partners, all talking at once.

Ask the first question, instructing them both to answer to each other. Allow three minutes.

Then, call time, and have the people in *one line only* move to the right one chair. The person on the right end leaves his or her seat, walks behind the line, and takes the vacated left end chair.

Ask the second question. Again, allow two or three minutes. Then, the same line moves to the right one more chair. Keep this going for five or six questions. Tell them if they finish before you call time to ask about each other's name tags. You could use the following questions. Consider making up some of your own.

1. How can people make you angry?
2. What is something you remember being punished for as a small child?
3. Tell each other about one of your proudest moments.

4. What is something you worry about?
5. Tell about an adult who has greatly influenced your life.
6. Tell about the best thing that happened to you this week.
7. What would you like to change about yourself?
8. What is something you are afraid of?
9. What is important to you in a friendship?
10. What is the worst thing a friend ever did to you?
11. What is something you wish you could do over?

This is a fun exercise, good for ice breaking, getting the youth (and leaders) used to opening their mouths and saying something. It gives the youth a chance to speak to the adults and vice versa. They are given a structured opportunity to talk to a person they might otherwise never speak to.

3) Introduce the process for planning. Display the newsprint sheet you have prepared with the purpose of youth ministry:

> Our goal is to be involved in the total life of our church and its ministry. The life of our congregation can be divided into the following categories:
>
> *Worship*
> *Study*
> *Ministry within the congregation*
> *Service (to the community)*
> *Fellowship*

Explain that in order to participate in the total life of the church, the youth group needs to decide on a variety of activities under each of the five categories. And they need to create a balance, so that they are not doing all study and recreation.

Also explain that they will be getting to know several adults in the church who are taking leadership roles in the five areas. At this point you can introduce the leaders and their respective areas.

Explain the procedure for planning. The group will divide into five smaller groups to discuss alternatives for activities in the five areas. Explain the rotation, which gives everyone a chance to visit all five areas twice (see pp. 73-74 for explanation). Explain that the adult leaders in the small groups have already listed a few ideas but will need to hear ideas from the youth. On the second rotation, the youth will indicate their top three or four favorite alternatives.

After the rotation everybody will come back to the total group to look at the choices. The leaders will briefly explain the top three choices in their areas.

Then you will put the top choices on the calendar, filling out your Sunday night structure (or whatever structure you have), perhaps using an occasional Saturday or weeknight and a couple of weekend overnights. You will try to balance the calendar with three or four choices from every category.

Explain that as soon as the activities and events are selected and placed on the calendar, *responsible persons* will be assigned to each activity. Responsible persons are youth "volunteers" who will help the leaders plan the activity. Usually two or three people are needed for each activity, event, mini-course, retreat, etc.

Note: Make sure the youth understand that the volunteer responsible persons are not the only ones involved in the activity. Believe it or not, a few youth will think that if they don't raise their hand to be a responsible person for a service project, they will be left out of that project.

You will be repeating the explanation of responsible persons when the time comes (see p. 75).

4) Divide into small groups. (Note: If you have less than ten people, you can accomplish this small group work of brainstorming and selecting activities as a total group. Start with Study and ask for suggestions to supplement those on the newsprint sheet. Then find the top three or four favorites. Do this with all five areas.)

After you have explained the planning process and introduced the leaders, divide the group into five smaller groups. Here is where the colored name tags come in. "All yellows go to this area, blues over there, pinks here," etc. Having the name tags be the directive for "who goes where" will save you the headache of having two friends begging to go to the same group. If there are any complaints, remind them that they will be rotating and visiting all the other areas.

In the small groups the area leaders have their first opportunity to "lead," to assist the young people in drawing up a list of activities in their particular category. These groups should be relaxed—sitting on floors, tables, chairs, whatever. We want our new adult leaders to feel as comfortable as possible in their first leadership role. Each group needs a felt pen and the sheet of newsprint prepared by the category leaders.

First, the leaders explain the few ideas they have listed. Then the youth are to add their own.

5) Rotation. After five minutes in these small groups, coordinators will call: "Rotate." Each small group moves on to the next area. The leaders explain the alternatives to this new group. The new kids add more ideas.

This is just a brainstorming session. Rotate again after five minutes.

After the groups have visited all five areas, call a

short break. The break is to give the leaders time to compare notes, to see if the activities are in the right category. Some, such as a prayer retreat, would be listed under more than one category.

Have everyone come together again as one group. Number off from one to five. Have all the ones go to the Worship area, twos to Study, etc. You now have new small groups. It is wise to make this regrouping. During the first rotation, one of the groups may have come up with an idea. They would tend to vote in a block the second time around. You are looking for individual preferences on this rotation.

During this rotation, the youth are to select their top three favorites in each category. The area leaders place a mark beside each choice. After five minutes, rotate. Have the next group prioritize—their top three choices.

By the time the rotation is completed, the leaders should have three or four top choices (the ones with the most votes) marked on their newsprint sheets.

6) *Break.* Time for chips, Cokes, etc. Leaders of the areas should bring their newsprint sheets to the wall for display. Tape all five side by side.

7) *Work on options and the calendar.* Place the calendar posterboards on the wall next to the newsprint sheets. Have the youth gather around where they can see the calendar and newsprint. Start right in looking at

the options for Study. Have one of the Study leaders briefly explain the top three choices. If the group is in agreement, go ahead and put them on the calendar. Then move on to Worship, etc.

Some choices will be easy to place. A Palm Sunday worship service would occur on Palm Sunday and most likely take two or three meetings for preparation. The three previous Sunday nights could be marked for this worship preparation.

A mini-course would need three or four consecutive sessions. Three Sunday nights in February may be a good choice. Hayride—late October? Camping—early May?

You will not have time to debate options on dates. Simply pick one and get it on the calendar. You will have forty-five minutes to cover the five categories. That is nine minutes per area. Some activities will be placed faster than others. Keep track of the time. Where you have a stalemate, ask for consensus and move on.

Call attention to special congregational events—special programs, mission emphasis week, stewardship, church picnic, etc. Also mention district or city-wide events. They need to be on the calendar.

Remember to set a date in January for a calendar check and evaluation. Also a date (a social) in May for evaluation, celebration, and plans for the summer. The whole leadership team will be involved in these two meetings of evaluation.

8) Assign responsible persons. This step is essential. If the youth happen to be getting restless or if you are losing their attention, stop. Resume the calendar later at the retreat, or break and come back to the calendar. Whatever, make sure you have enough time (fifteen to twenty minutes) to get everyone signed up as responsible persons.

Explain again what a responsible person does. For each activity, event, mini-course, there need to be two or three youth to work with the category leaders in the planning and the preparation of the event, to help gather materials and to take leadership roles. The leaders and responsible persons will arrange to meet a month before their scheduled activity to begin planning, to decide what needs to be done in preparation. This meeting may take only twenty minutes and could be scheduled immediately following a regular meeting.

Everyone needs to sign up for at least one activity. Most likely (unless you have forty-five or more in your youth group) they will sign up for more than one. Encourage those who are reluctant to speak up to sign up for such and such. You don't want to embarrass anyone, but you may need to use "gentle coercion." If you have a few spaces open, great. Save them for those youth who could not make it to the planning retreat. Catch them next week at the follow-up meeting. Phone them this week.

Make sure you put the names down on the newsprint. Tell the group that you will send them copies of the calendar with the names of responsible persons, so that everyone will know what is happening when and for which activities they agreed to be responsible.

Note: During the year, some young persons may need to change their responsibilities. That is okay. They have not signed their lives away at the planning retreat. We want them to take responsibility, but we don't want to come down hard on them. If they need to back out, then see what can be worked out. They might switch with someone. Remember, you are trying to build good relationships.

Tell everybody to get their friends who did not make the retreat to come to the next meeting, for you will be going over the calendar and signing more responsible persons.

And so ends the planning part of the retreat. It is time for fun, recreation, singing, whatever.

If, at the end of the planning, you feel a little confused, don't get discouraged. The program will begin to make sense when you carry out these follow-up items:

(a) Checking out details of activities chosen. Checking out specific dates.
(b) Spending the next meeting going over the calendar and involving new youth as responsible persons.
(c) Reproducing the calendar and the list of responsible persons.

Other Aspects of the Retreat

For the best suggestions on carrying out any retreat, I highly recommend the *Retreat Handbook: A–Way to Meaning* by Virgil and Lynn Nelson (Judson Press). I personally have always been pro structure when it comes to retreats. Retreats offer the kind of time needed to effectively build community within a group. To be effective, we need to plan carefully the way we will use

the time. Too much free time encourages the smaller "cliques" of friends to go off on their own. Those who are not "in" with the smaller circles are left out.

Bringing Friends

Have you ever had a young person ask, "Can I bring a friend?" to a retreat? This is most common and for a logical reason. Bringing a friend insures that the young person will have a good time. He or she needs that security, especially if most of the kids there will have their own circle of friends.

Whenever our kids "bring friends" to a retreat, we make sure everyone knows that the friend may be in another small group when we break for small group activities. We want everyone to know why, and that is because everybody should have a chance to get to know each other. This helps the group become a group, one in which all can enjoy being with a variety of personalities.

Sample Schedules

The following schedules are outlines with suggestions to guide you in planning the retreat. The activities are described in Appendix C. Of course you are encouraged to find other options for activities.

Saturday-Sunday (one night)

Saturday

12:15 — Lunch

1:00 — Ice breakers and get-acquainted games:
Introduction Interview (App. C, no. 1)
(works well with a mixture of adults and youth)
John, John, John (no. 8)
Zip, Zap (no. 7)

1:45 — Outdoor recreation:
volleyball, softball, football, New Games (ch. 17, no. 21)

3:30 — Free time

4:30 — Group games:
Name Charade (no. 13)
One Frog (no. 16)
Grand Prix Race (no. 17)

6:00 — Supper

7:00 — Group singing *(before or after supper)*:

There seem to be times when singing as a group works more naturally than others. Try to get a feel for when singing will be most enjoyable. A group of reluctant singers is deadly!

7:30 — The planning process

10:30 — Break

11:00 — Break into small groups of 4 or 5 persons each.
Open-ended statements:

If I could have lunch with a famous person, it would be . . .
My favorite thing to do on a vacation is . . .
If I were in the circus, I would be the . . .

Four Facts/One Lie (no. 20)
Each person could design a skit for late presentation.

12:00 — Games *(combine smaller groups to make groups of 8 to 12)*:
A What? (no. 15)
Operant Conditioning (no. 32)

12:45 — Break

1:15 — Do skits.
Make movies *(if someone has an 8mm camera)*.
Show a movie *(16mm, ordered ahead)*.
Sing.
(whatever leaders and kids are still game for)

I like to make good use of the late hours at a retreat. For some reason, people seem to feel closer to each other as the hours wear on. Have a late "lights out" and then serve breakfast at 9:00 A.M. (not the crack of dawn).

Sunday

9:00 — Breakfast

9:30 — Prepare for worship in groups *(see p. 78 for a design in which the youth create their own worship service)*

11:00 — Worship

11:45 — Clean up, pack up

12:30 — Lunch and final cleanup

Friday-Saturday-Sunday

A two-night retreat could include more in-depth group building, and Bible study relating to the theme of caring, or being a community, or the church. A schedule might look like this:

Friday night

6:30 — Supper *(or supper en-route)*

7:30 — Ice breakers:

Introduction Interview (App. C, no. 1)
Zip Zap (no. 7)

In small groups of four to six:

Open-ended statements (no. 23)
Four Facts/One Lie (no. 20)
A Special Dinner (no. 22)

8:30 — Break

8:45 — Group games and recreation
(refer to preceding retreat schedule for suggestions and to chapter 17 for related books)

10:00 — A movie or singing

10:45 — Goofy games:

Grand Prix Race (no. 17)
One Frog (no. 16)

Values exercises make fun activities, even when they are unrelated to a value process course. See nos. 18, 21-23, 29-31, also chapter 17, no. 36.

12:00 — Midnight vespers (could have been prepared by a group of responsible persons and a leader)
Singing
Anything else (play it by ear)

Saturday

9:00 — Breakfast

9:30 — The planning process

12:30 — Lunch
Free time

2:00 — Outdoor games and recreation

4:30 — Free time

5:00 — Group games:

Name Charade (no. 13)
Guess Who? (no. 19)

6:00 — Supper

7:00 — Singing

7:30 — Break into small groups to work on worship for Sunday morning (p. 78)

8:30 — Break

9:00 — Bible study in small groups (4-6 each):

Each group does a different method, then comes together to share product (see p. 111).

9:45 — Games:
Operant Conditioning (no. 32)
A What? (no. 15)

10:30 — Break

11:00 — Could do skits, a movie, singing

12:00 — Midnight vespers (prepared ahead by group of youth and leaders)
A good game of crab soccer (no. 34) will almost guarantee sleep, which is necessary on a two-night retreat.

Encourage bedtime earlier this night.

Sunday

9:00 — Breakfast

9:30 — Small groups finish worship preparation

11:00 — Worship

11:45 — Clean up, pack up

12:30 — Lunch and final cleanup

These schedules are not meant to be inflexible. Some activities will take longer than you expected. Others shorter. You may get to a point in the evening where you feel your planned item is not appropriate. Be flexible. Have other activities on hand for a change of pace.

Sleep

Sleep is not an absolute necessity on a one-night retreat. It is on a two-night retreat. Thus, an early (or earlier) bedtime is encouraged. I usually do not enforce bedtimes, except in the sleeping area. In other words, those who want to stay up should have a room designated as the "stay awake" room. It should be far enough away from the sleepers so as not to disturb them. Of course, it should not be a mile away from the group either, nor in the woods.

Agreeing on the Guidelines

Everybody should know what the "rules" or guidelines are. The youth should be aware of these *before* going on the retreat. The youth need reasonable limits in which to function.

First, there's the "Big Three": no alcohol, no drugs, no sex. Then there is one very important rule which you ask the youth to agree to, and that is:

> Everyone is to participate in all the planned activities.

Discuss this with them before you go. Include it in the letter which advises them what to bring, where to meet, etc.

The youth will also need to know where they can go (and where they cannot go) for free time and for staying up late.

Beyond these, the only rules will be those made by the camp facility which you are using. Go over these with the youth, emphasizing the need to abide by the rules of the place in which you are guests.

All Adult Leaders: Know the Guidelines!

Coordinators: Go over the guidelines with the leadership team at your last training session or upon arrival at the retreat site. The adult leaders need to know the limits and rules, as well as the schedule, so they won't give different answers to questions the youth will ask.

Enforcing the Guidelines

There can be a problem here. Many of the adult leaders will be new with the kids. They may feel uncomfortable playing the "heavy," as in retrieving kids from the bushes or asking the late-nighters to keep it down for the seventh time. On the other hand, there are adults who don't mind playing the "heavy" (at least once-in-a-while).

Coordinators: Talk this over at the training sessions. Your team may expect you to be the enforcer. And your expectations are that all leaders share in this role. With all your responsibilities, you may need their help in this area. Make sure this is clarified.

Every adult on the leadership team should understand his or her role throughout the retreat.

Recreation

I am by no means an expert on games and recreation. The best materials I have seen are: the *Retreat Handbook* by Virgil and Lynn Nelson (chapter 17, no. 19); *Guide for Recreation Leaders* by Glenn Bannerman and Robert Fakkema (no. 20); and *The New Games Book: Play Hard, Play Fair, Nobody Hurt,* edited by Andrew Fluegelman (no. 21).

Worship

A retreat provides a good setting and the kind of time needed for youth to design their own worship experience. Usually a small group is responsible for preparing the service of worship. The problem with this method is that all the youth don't have a part in creating the experience.

After experimenting with several ideas, we found one method which does involve *all* the youth at the retreat. They choose the theme, work on all the elements, and put it together.

This method may give you ideas as to how to involve your group in designing their own worship.

Choosing the Theme.

1) To the entire group, we showed a variety of slides (no one theme was represented). We have been collecting slides over the years for use in various multimedia productions. Some were taken by our own amateur photographers. Others are from commercial sources, such as Mark IV and TeleSLIDES. (See chapter 17 for addresses of these sources.)

Some slides were symbolic, impressionistic. Others were of people, places, buildings, money, food—a wide variety of things. The youth were given paper and pencils and were instructed to write down a feeling they had as each slide was shown, a word for each slide.

2) We divided into small groups of seven or eight youth and adult leaders. Each group was to discuss the feelings they had relating to specific pictures. They were asked: "Which pictures stood out in your mind?"

After discussion, they were to suggest several themes which they saw through the slides. Then they

were to choose a theme around which to develop a service of worship.

3) Everybody came back together. We listed on newsprint each group's theme suggestion. From this list the kids voted on one theme. This was to be the theme of their worship experience.

Creating the Worship Experience. To work on the individual parts of the service, we divided into smaller groups. Each person worked on one of the following:

1. Call to Worship and Benediction
2. Prayer of Confession, Assurance of Pardon
3. Hymns or Songs
4. Prayer—Petition, Thanksgiving, Intercession
5. Scripture
6. Proclamation of the Word

The small groups were encouraged to use a variety of methods in creating the various parts:

litany, responsive reading   creative writing
slides   creative movement
music

The preparation took about an hour and a half.

We did little to coordinate the parts. Thus, we did not have a "polished" service. But both times we have used this design we have been very pleased with the results. The parts fit together better than we expected.

More important, though, was the youth reaction. They enjoyed it. They were involved in the worship. They evaluated it as very meaningful. It was obvious that it was their creation. They were much more responsive than if we or a small group had planned the experience for everybody.

Coordinators: "Walk through" every activity, every part of the retreat schedule. Write down materials you will need for each part. Envision the activities taking place. This will help you prepare for possible difficulties. For example, you are planning to pop popcorn. By "walking through," you discover you need to consider how you are going to distribute the popcorn to 75 people. You need some kind of containers.

"Walking through" saves time and frustration.

Make sure you keep all the newsprint sheets (with responsible persons listed) and the calendars.

Note: In one of those free time slots you might get your leaders together for an evaluation. Plan to evaluate the whole retreat at a later time.

11
Follow-up to the Planning Retreat

During the week between the Planning Retreat and the follow-up planning meeting, coordinators should examine the calendars, making notes on questions which need answers. Several of the dates will need checking. For example, if the youth are planning to have a short Advent candlelighting service during worship on the four Sundays in Advent, you will definitely need to check that out. If you have scheduled a drama for Wednesday night supper or a pancake breakfast, make sure you check with ministers, directors of Christian education, or whomever.

Discuss the calendar with the category leaders. You certainly don't want to plan a major Fellowship event when the Fellowship leaders are out of town. The more you can check out in this next week, the more accurate your calendar will be. Go ahead and make the necessary changes. Then check them out with the youth at the follow-up meeting.

Getting Youth to the Follow-up Meeting

Undoubtedly, there will be many youth who could not attend the retreat, both regulars and "ne'er go near the church door-ers." This is the week to make the big push to get them on board. Tell the youth to talk with these kids at school and get them out to the follow-up meeting. Coordinators (and leaders who feel comfortable doing so) should call all the kids who were not at the retreat. Let them know that the youth are in the process of planning the year and you want them to have the opportunity to get in on it, to offer ideas, and to join in as responsible persons (which "everybody else" is doing).

And the Leaders

Coordinators: Call those leaders on the team who were unable to be at the planning retreat right away. This will let them know that they are important members of the team, that you have been thinking about them and need to fill them in on details of the retreat. Make sure they understand that they are needed at the follow-up meeting. Go over the activities and dates selected in their categories.

The Follow-up Meeting

The setting for this meeting can be almost anything you wish, except another retreat. It could be a regular schedule-type meeting, i.e., 6:00-7:30 Sunday night. Or you may be having a fun night supper in someone's home. Whatever, give yourself forty-five minutes in which to go over the calendar and involve responsible persons. Begin the session with fifteen minutes of group builders. Check with some of the youth who were at the retreat. They may have a couple of favorites from the retreat to try with the other kids. See "Group-Building Activities," Appendix C.

Briefly explain how the planning proceeded and display the newsprint sheets from all five categories with the priorities checked. Display the calendar and go over the months of activities.

Explain details, confirmed dates, and changes which you coordinators checked out during the week. Ask for suggestions for activities which then can be negotiated by the entire group.

Point out the spaces which need to be filled by new responsible persons. Try to get all the youth to take a responsible person role. Hopefully, you can get a reasonable balance, for several youth will no doubt have signed up for six or seven items.

Announce that everyone will receive copies of the calendars, with their names underlined. They will need to know when their responsibilities are coming around.

Evaluate

Spend a few minutes looking over the planned year. Ask the youth to evaluate. Do we have balance? Are we doing a variety of activities in each and every category?

Ask them what was good about the planning. What was not so good? What was the weakest part of the planning process? How might we do it differently—to improve it? Jot down their responses on newsprint. Or appoint a recorder to write down the suggestions.

Do take seriously their responses. Consider incorporating their suggestions in next year's planning or for midyear planning.

Parent Involvement

You either have had a Parent Night or are planning to have one soon. Give the youth a chance to brainstorm ideas they have for involving the parents during the year (see chapter 9).

After the Follow-up Meeting

Check on details in an effort to establish a fairly accurate calendar. You should now be able to place the activities permanently on the posterboard calendar. Transfer them from your acetate or kitchen wrap covering, or pen them in neatly on the clear-stick covering (if that is what you have used on the posterboards).

Display the calendars somewhere in the church building where they can be seen by a majority of the church membership. Don't put them up in the youth rooms. We are aiming for visibility of this ambitious youth program. So, put the calendars where people can see what is happening in youth ministry at their church.

Send Out Calendars to All Youth

Reproduce the calendar on a stencil, listing the activities, the names of related adult leaders, and the responsible persons. You can find examples of calendars on pages 12 and 82.

Personalize each calendar. When you are getting ready to mail a calendar to Sara Smith, underline in red ink Sara's name each time it appears on the calendar. Also, underline the activity and circle the date. This will alert Sara to her responsible role and let her know when those activities are coming up.

Do the same for the adult leaders. Underline their names, activities, and circle the dates. The leadership team members need to know when they are going to "lead."

Try to get this calendar out in the next week. If you put it off, it will be taken less seriously by both the youth and the adult leaders.

You might want to send the calendars to parents and other interested adults. Check with the youth. If you are having a Parent Night soon, plan to distribute the calendars to parents at that time.

Once the calendar is visible—both in the hands of the youth and up in view of the congregation—then you will begin to feel like youth ministry is really happening. It is underway. You have direction, strategy, resources, and leadership. Something is happening with youth at your church!

Senior High Calendar

Dates	Program	Adult Leaders	Responsible Persons
Oct. 8 15	Worship workshop	Herb Gale	
22 29	Work on haunted house Haunted house	Pete Gilbert, Mabel Lampley	Chuck Lampley, Laura Arrowood
31	UNICEF collecting	Pete Gilbert, Mabel Lampley	Laura Dixon, Maree McCants
Nov. 5 12 19	Study: Book of Revelation	Sid Dixon, Bill Drumwright	Alan Monteith, Jeff Leonell
26 Dec. 3 10	Work on Christmas play and Advent worship	Larry Green Bud & Sandy Leopard	Lisa Reynolds, Ruth Whetstone
17	Hayride/Christmas caroling	Ed & Edna Patterson George & Susan Doggett	Laura Dixon, Laura Arrowood
20	Present Christmas play	Larry Greer, Bud & Sandy Leopard	Lisa Reynolds, Ruth Whetstone
24	Christmas Eve service (no youth group meeting)		
31	No meeting		
Jan. 7 14	Youth Problems: dating, sexuality, etc.	Sid Dixon, Bill Drumwright	Greg Myers, Linda Myers, Linda Beard
19-21	Retreat on Sexuality (*Your Values* *and Your Sex*)	Ed & Edna Patterson George & Susan Doggett	
28	Open		
Feb. 4	Progressive dinner	Ed & Edna Patterson, George & Susan Doggett	Harvey Hamrick, Dorothy Hamrick, Laura Arrowood
11	Clown ministry workshop	Pete Gilbert, Mabel Lampley	Linda Myers, Laura Arrowood, Lisa Reynolds
18	Volleyball	Ed & Edna Patterson, George & Susan Doggett	
25	Prepare for cold camping	Ed & Edna Patterson George & Susan Doggett	Harvey Hamrick, Chuck Lampley
Mar. 4	Cook your own dinner in youth lounge/Prepare for cold camping		
9-11	Cold camping		
18	Open		
25	Progressive dinner	Ed & Edna Patterson, George & Susan Doggett	Harvey Hamrick, Dorothy Hamrick, Laura Arrowood
Apr. 1	Open		
8 15 22	Study: Death and Life After Death	Sid Dixon, Bill Drumwright	Wendy Pharr, Elena Patterson
29	Cookout at someone's house	Ed & Edna Patterson, George & Susan Doggett	Laura Dixon, Linda Myers
May 6 13	Prepare for worship service on May 20	Larry Greer, Bud & Sandy Leopard	Laura Dixon, Dorothy Hamrick, Chuck Lampley
20	Morning: Youth lead worship service Night: Open		
27	Talk about Montreat Youth Conference		

12
Throughout the Year

You are off and running. The year is planned. If you have pushed to get as many youth as possible involved at the start of the year, then you should have a good group, as well as a good "program." A lot of energy goes into getting youth ministry going. Now what does it take to keep it going throughout the year? In the Coordinators' Chapter and in the Leaders' Chapter, I have explained the responsibilities of the leadership team. The coordinators will carry the burden of overseeing youth ministry throughout the year. In addition to these responsibilities, everybody involved should work at building enthusiasm for youth ministry and interpreting youth ministry to the congregation.

Communicating

The greatest problem you will face during the year will be in the area of communication. Here is where breakdown can occur. Coordinators need to be in constant communication with each other, handling a variety of details and being aware of needed resources. Staying ahead is the challenge.

Coordinators: Watch the calendar. Call respective leaders a month ahead to remind them of upcoming activities. Keep asking them questions: "Will you need help getting materials, resources, or arranging for certain activities?" Or just: "Do you need help?" The tendency is to let things slide and then on Saturday night, give a call to the next night's leaders, asking if everything is set up.

One advantage of having two leaders per category is that you have two people aware of the calendar, one of whom will likely make that phone call to the other: "Hey, we've got to get going on this." You also have youth leadership, responsible persons, who are invaluable, but who will probably not be thinking ahead.

Encourage the youth to watch the calendar, reminding each other of what is coming up. The youth won't want to have any of their activities canceled because nobody did anything until the last minute.

Do all you can, coordinators, leaders, and youth, to keep each other on top of the program. Get details straight, especially if any changes are made. When changes in dates, location, or whatever are made, use all means of communiction and publicity to get the right word out.

Have a special mailbox or boxes (manila envelopes hung somewhere) for your leadership team. This helps keep the team informed, for they can check their boxes each Sunday. Pass on resources that should be shared by all team members.

See that the leadership team members get on mailing lists, such as presbytery/district and denominational mailing lists.

Publicity

Involve the youth as much as you can in publicity efforts. You might appoint a publicity person (adult or youth) to see that publicity happens. The responsible persons for each activity should work out a strategy for publicizing that activity. Explore all the possible means of publicity in your church:

1) *Bulletins, announcements/congregational concerns* at worship services.

2) *Newsletters.* Have a youth section in your monthly or bimonthly newsletter. This could be written by a team of youth or adults and youth. Consider a youth newsletter quarterly. Include articles from church school classes, scouts, choirs, etc. It could also have creative writings by youth and editorials on issues in the church or community. In each issue you could do

a profile on one of the leadership team adults. Use it to publicize local, presbytery/district, and denominational events.

3) Posters. Make posters to publicize upcoming events.

4) Bulletin boards. Have a youth bulletin board, with space for other items besides the calendars. Use photographic displays of youth ministry—your youth involved in the life of the church, in all aspects of its ministry. You could do five displays at different times during the year, each explaining the five different areas in youth ministry.

5) Fliers. Periodically send home fliers publicizing events—special worship, a mini-course, a trip, service project. Put a stack of these fliers in the narthex and in an area of the church school wing or near the church office where all members of the congregation can pick them up.

6) Brochure. Consider putting out a brochure sometime during the year, designed by the youth, publicizing youth ministry.

7) Media. Plan a slide production publicizing youth ministry in your church. Have the youth do the camera work and write the script. Such a five-to-ten-minute production could be used at congregational gatherings—suppers, picnics, retreats, or during stewardship season.

All these methods of publicity will be necessary, not only to keep communication lines open among leaders and youth, but to communicate youth ministry to the congregation.

Interpreting Youth Ministry to the Congregation

This book does not advocate a fancy youth program for the sake of the youth. Rather, what we in youth ministry are about is offering youth opportunities to play a vital role in the life of the church. We have been talking strategy for activating youth to such a role. But we will find ourselves stymied if we do not work at advocating and interpreting youth ministry to the local congregation.

All that has been mentioned above under publicity should be used as part of a strategy to communicate and interpret youth ministry to the congregation.

In chapter 3 I explained the need to communicate this new leadership team approach to the congregation. We talked about involving and getting the support of the staff—ministers, directors of Christian education, and the policymaking board. Their support is crucial, both to the introduction of this concept and to the development of youth ministry throughout the year

and in years to come. If you happened to bypass this crucial step when you were starting out, now is the time to work at getting this support.

In the beginning we work at building enthusiasm for youth ministry. That enthusiasm will not be sustained unless we, coordinators, leaders, and youth, initiate a plan of action throughout the year.

Publicity and the advertising of upcoming events is only part of this process. The congregation needs to know the "why" of what we are doing in youth ministry. This involves:

1. Statements of purpose periodically
2. Visibility of our youth in ministry
3. Advocating youth concerns

Statements of What We Are About in Youth Ministry

Through the same avenues mentioned under publicity, we need to continually make statements about youth ministry—describing the increasing involvement of adults, proclaiming the good news through the efforts of our youth, and exploring the meaning of the community of faith and the role of youth in that community. This task should be on the agenda of every meeting of the leadership team. Where can we make statements of the meaning of our ministry with and of the youth?

As responsible persons and leaders meet to plan upcoming activities, they need to evaluate the meaning of the entire program. Does the congregation know what we are doing and why? It will take some brainstorming of ideas and methods on how to communicate to the congregation what is happening with our youth.

Visibility of the Youth

Whatever the activity and wherever possible, our youth should be seen. If they are serving a dinner or collecting canned goods for needy families, the youth should be seen by the rest of the congregation. Even if it only takes a few kids to do a job, the rest of the group should be there, visible.

For example, if the junior highs are leading a fun night for a congregational gathering, it may take only five youth to actually lead, but the rest should be there, visible, participating up front. If the senior highs are doing a children's sermon during Sunday morning worship, three may have speaking parts, but the rest of the group should be up front too. The children and adults need to know the youth. If the junior highs are doing a drama, those not in the cast should be visible at some point.

Someone suggested T-shirts for visibility and as a means of identification. T-shirts could be printed for all youth, with the name of the youth group, or even just

the name of your church, or—c'mon, creative people—someone can think up a good design for a T-shirt.

The visibility of the adult leaders is equally important. Every member of the congregation should be able to tell a visitor who works with the youth in the church, which, in this case, means he or she would rattle off a list of names. Rather impressive to an outsider.

Get the names of the leadership team, as well as their faces, before the congregation. Just this year we have printed T-shirts saying: "I am on the Youth Ministry Team at Shelby Presbyterian Church." The leaders wear them frequently—at church picnics, retreats, recreation activities.

A special program related to youth ministry or youth concerns may be in order if you have regular weeknight congregational suppers or fellowship gatherings. Plan an activity which acquaints the congregation with the leadership team, something more than a simple introduction. Perhaps a takeoff on a popular television show or game show, a skit, or even a talent show by the adult leaders (the kind where wiggling your ears is a talent).

Advocating Youth and Their Concerns

Youth are not quite capable of speaking for themselves and for issues concerning them. They need adults who will speak for them and with them as advocates. I would like to see one adult take on the role of "Youth Advocate." He or she would be a member of the session or board whose function would be to keep up with youth in 19__. This person may or may not be a category leader, but would be a part of the leadership team. Such people would read everything they could get their hands on relating to adolescence and especially to youth in their present culture. This person would keep up with what is happening in the schools, would know where youth go and what is available in the community for youth.

The youth advocate would voice youth concerns to the session or board. This would have to be a person who is thoroughly interested in youth, one who would recognize the needs of young people and be able to relate those needs to the congregation.

Most of you will not have a full-time "youth-advocate." Therefore, all the adults on the leadership team should perform this function. There will be certain leaders more capable and more interested in advocating youth concerns than others.

Coordinators: Find out who these people are. Discuss with them ways of advocating. I like to see a member of the session or board on the adult leadership team. This person can be the liaison needed for keeping youth ministry a high priority.

Advocating is a crucial part of interpreting youth ministry to the congregation. Too many people today misunderstand youth. Some adults fear them. Others merely tolerate them until they are "older and know better." Others think they are children and therefore treat them as second-class, "junior" church members. Educating a congregation about youth is a big undertaking, one which takes a lot of effort and patience.

I would like to see churches have youth ministry workshops, not for advisors and potential leaders, but for the general populace, for everybody who has any interest in knowing about young people today. Many parents would be interested. The content of such a workshop could deal with a variety of topics: the culture and today's youth; the effect of television and other electronic media on young people; possibilities for ministry by our youth; youth and the Christian faith; youth—transition from childhood to adulthood; youth in the job market. I could see part of this workshop being taught by a few youth or by a team of youth and adults.

I would also like to see a class offered on the presbytery/district level or at denominational conferences for church officers on how to relate to youth and involve them on church boards, committees, and task forces.

One of the most pressing needs of youth that our congregations should understand is their need for affirmation and recognition. Youth need to be affirmed. They need to feel the support of their church family in all they do. This takes time to cultivate. Youth also need recognition, but not the first grade style—"Aren't we proud of our young people?" Rather, they need recognition that says, "We take you seriously." We want visibility of our youth, but not the kind where we display them before the congregation, and everyone applauds sweetly as we march them off the stage.

We adult leaders must teach the congregation how to affirm our youth. Here is where intergenerational activities play an important role. The essential ingredient in all curriculum and other materials written for generations working and playing together is that each age group is taken seriously. Children, youth, and adults work side by side with equal importance.

Be on the lookout for intergenerational opportunities. If they are not structured into this year's calendar, make note of that in evaluation and encourage the youth to consider more intergenerational activities next year, or during the summer. In many churches the summer provides a break from routine. Church school programs try intergenerational situations. Special summer events are designed for participation by all ages.

Another way we leaders can teach the congregation how to affirm and recognize our youth is by being examples ourselves. Our investment of time, energy, enthusiasm, and interest with youth will be seen. It would be hard not to recognize the interest and enthusism of twenty to twenty-four adult leaders. The congregation will see how seriously we take youth and youth ministry.

Be aware of how your relationship with the youth comes across to the church family. If you feel like you are merely leading youth by taking their hands and walking them through activities, then a red flag should go up. Perhaps you are underestimating the capabilities of the youth. Work with other leaders on the team, evaluting how the program is coming across. Are the youth involved in activities which are important, which affirm them, and which can be recognized as vital to their experience within the church community?

One last word on interpreting youth ministry to the congregation: make sure in your strategy that you are spreading your efforts over the entire year. Youth ministry needs to be constantly before the congregation—visible and vital.

Youth Ministry: The New Team Approach

Evaluation

Probably the most helpful tool for carrying out youth ministry during the year is evaluation. The leadership team needs to take a look periodically at how things are going. The youth need to do this too.

— What have we done well? And why has it worked well?

— What is not working so well? Discuss reasons why not. What should we do differently?

— How do the leaders feel about their particular roles? Do they feel supported? What could the church do to better support them?

— Are the responsible persons working? If not, why not? Perhaps leaders are not calling on them.

— What about the participation by the youth? Is it meaningful? Are they increasingly becoming a real part of the church community?

— Is the church taking the young people seriously? Are they being affirmed, recognized?

— Are we communicating with each other? Where is it breaking down?

— Are we making progress in interpreting youth ministry to the congregation?

Every time you evaluate, or whenever you hear comments from youth, leaders, parents, or other church members, take good notes and share the comments with the leadership team. The more you evaluate and work with ideas and suggestions, the more confidence you will gain as leaders and coordinators. Working together, you will see a vital youth ministry develop within your church community.

13
Adapting to Varieties of Situations

If you have made it through the basics of this leadership team approach, I hope you are not overwhelmed. The question you are undoubtedly asking is, How will this work in my church? or even, Will it work in my church? At first glance, one might think this concept is only for large churches, or that you have to have a full-time youth director to run it. Let me assure you that the leadership team approach was not designed for the large church. In fact, it may not be the best model for churches of 2,000 or more members. If those churches succeeded in attaining the involvement of all their youth in every aspect of the church's life, they would need to go beyond what this model offers.

The Large Church

Large churches have the same problem as small and middle-size—low youth involvement. Large churches too are crying out for help to motivate their youth to be "active." For those churches, this approach can be a starting point. Surely the potential for adult leadership is greater in a larger church, although you do have the problem of knowing who these adults are. And it may take longer to find them.

Once the adults are found, it would be an asset for a large church to have a youth ministry team. It would be incredibly hard for two or three advisors to build youth ministry all by themselves. Large churches need people power to relate to all those young people on the church roll.

After four or five years of using the leadership team approach, the large church will hopefully have so many youth involved that it will need to branch out, going to a more diversified program. Adults would be recruited to highly specialized areas of the youth ministry program —drama, photography, music, publicity, welcome wagon (visitation), social services, clown ministry, sports teams (leagues), in-depth study groups. With such an expanded program, there would be opportunities for youth to lead in some of these areas.

The Small Church

The majority of churches across all denominations are small. It is to you in small churches that I would like to describe how this approach can be used. When you read the part about twenty to twenty-four adults actively involved in youth ministry, was your reaction: "That's more people than we have working in every leadership situation in the entire church program!"?

Way back when I was first thinking about this concept, I was receiving calls from small churches asking for help in the youth area. I was concerned about whether this concept would be of any value. So I introduced it to a youth ministry class at the Smaller Church Conference at Montreat, North Carolina in 1977, expecting to be laughed at. I was surprised to find that they not only accepted the concept, but they (youth advisors from churches of 200 or less members) came up with great ideas for adapting this approach to their own churches.

You who are in smaller churches are the best equipped to adapt this concept to your own situation. I will share with you ideas I have received from others in similar small church situations.

First of all, it may help to reemphasize that the adults on the leadership team will have time to work in other areas of the church's life. In the small church it is

usually necessary for church members to wear more than one hat. Community and interdependency seem to come more naturally in the small church, especially in the small rural church, where everybody must "pitch in" in order for the church to survive. In these churches individuals find themselves taking various leadership roles and participating in many aspects of ministry. A member of the youth ministry team can, during the same year, be a church school teacher or a member of a committee. The adults you are recruiting need to know that they will likely be asked to participate in other leadership roles.

Also, let me reassure you that the number of adults on the youth ministry team will not overwhelm your small junior high group of six. Only two adults will be with them at any one time. (If you have five or less possible young people in your church, I strongly suggest getting together with another church. See p. 90.)

Consider Combining Categories

The structure of this approach can be modified to fit your particular situation through the combining of categories. We have discovered that Worship and Ministry Within the Congregation combine well. Service

and Ministry Within the Congregation may be combined, but you would have to be careful that one does not become lost in the other. Youth can have projects in which they rake leaves for members of the church, serve special dinners, and work with the elderly. These would usually be considered "service." However, none of these relates to service to the community (outside the congregation). Likewise, kids could have service projects and not have the opportunities to be involved with other members of the congregation.

Note: If you do combine categories, the leaders who are recruited need to understand that they are taking double responsibility. At the planning retreat, they will need to make two sheets, one for each category. The youth will still choose three or four activities in each category. The combined category leaders are responsible for six to eight activities, not the usual three or four.

One Adult per Category

Another modification would be to recruit one adult leader per category. This cuts the personnel in half. Talk with prospective leaders about this possibility. I have heard many say that they need the team emphasis for each category. They don't want to take on their category alone. There is greater support when two do it. You will need to take this into consideration.

Need to Involve Youth

I recommend this approach for small churches because too often the smaller church has a mind-set of "small" youth program. "All we can offer our youth is study and recreation." If that is the way most of your folks seem to think, then you need to clue them in that the small church community is an ideal setting for a broader youth ministry. For example, encouraging Ministry Within the Congregation in the small church is not difficult, because most everybody in the congregation knows each other. You will need to work at Worship and Service. It is often hard to find Service opportunities in a small community.

Combining Junior and Senior Highs

Should you combine junior and senior high groups? A common question. Answer: Not unless absolutely necessary. There is a definite difference in these age groups. Granted, ninth graders could be in either group. But there is a vast difference between the seventh and the twelfth grader. Some groups include sixth graders, which makes age difference even more of a problem.

What you usually have in a combined group is a happy group of younger adolescents who love being able to do what the older kids get to do, and some miserable eleventh and twelfth graders who cannot stand having the younger ones around.

Before I would combine junior and senior highs into one group, my inclination would be to look for an ecumenical possibility. I would try to find another church with the same problem and combine, so that we could have a junior high group and a separate senior high group.

If, for whatever reason, you must combine, you can still use the leadership team concept. You would have one team of ten to twelve adults. Be sensitive in planning, for there may be activities suggested which are more appropriate for younger adolescents. Let the younger ones do it. Same for the older kids. For example, the older ones may want to do a sexuality study retreat with their own age group. Let them. The younger ones may want a dance. Let them invite all their friends and have a junior high dance.

There may be problems choosing study options in a combined group. If all are to participate in the same mini-course or topic, make sure you use the small group method a lot. This means that after you introduce the topic, at some point you would divide them into their age groups for discussion or activities related to the topic. If you must work with all ages (seventh through twelfth grades), keep your eyes open for opportunities to split them into junior and senior high groups, whether it be for a study, a service project, participation in worship, whatever. It will keep both age extremes interested and motivated.

Evaluate what you are doing in a combined junior/ senior high group. The "rule of thumb" is the wider the age span, the greater the need for a wider variety of activities. You need the variety in order to meet the needs of the various ages in your group.

Ecumenical Relationships

Many churches are finally getting rid of their insecurity complex which requires them to have their own successful youth group before being willing to venture off and communicate with youth groups from other denominations.

I recall suggesting to one church that they combine their youth group with another small church. The response was a definite no. "We have to build our own First Church youth group. Get our kids involved and active first, then we might consider joint ventures." That church couldn't draw those few kids out and motivate them to "be active." There were too few young people. If they could have united with the other church in youth ministry, chances are the excitement of the new venture would have attracted the young people.

Many small churches are joining together in youth ministry. They are realizing the potential, not only in increased numbers of youth, but in increased adult leadership possibilities.

I like to see youth exposed to other church and faith traditions. Our kids know very little about their own denomination. Why am I a Presbyterian? a Baptist? a Lutheran? By being exposed to other denominations, the young people are beginning to take interest—hey, just why am I a Presbyterian? a Baptist? a Catholic?

In practice, an ecumenical youth group has an adult leadership team of ten to twelve adults for junior highs and ten to twelve for senior highs. They come from all participating churches. The process is quite the same. The youth choose three or four activities in each category. What is different concerns Worship and Ministry Within the Congregation. If, for example, the youth choose to participate in a Sunday morning worship, they may have to split up and do what they plan in their own services. Or, they can take their planned worship experience and repeat it for each of the participating denominations.

Care must be taken in Ministry Within the Congregation to see that the young people are given opportunities to be involved in their own congregations, with adults and children at their own churches. And yet you want to give the kids exposure to each other's church life. Where possible, involve all the youth in a congregational activity. But, also make sure each congregation sees and knows its own youth.

The Larger Youth Ministry Team

The concept of an even larger youth ministry team than the leadership team presented in this book is recommended and suggested in chapter 14. My ideal of youth ministry would be a team of adults and youth who have leadership roles in every area of the church's life that involves youth. The larger youth ministry team would include church school teachers of all youth classes, scout leaders of church troops, youth choir directors, handbell and other instrumental directors, and other youth advocates (such as a Young Life leader, if he or she is a member of your church, and any junior or senior high school teachers in your congregation) who could be recruited to serve on a youth ministry team. Youth would be on the team on a rotating basis.

I do not recommend this large a team for your first year with this concept for the obvious reason: the leadership team approach is confusing enough with twenty to twenty-four adults. Get it started and going, and then, in the second or third year, pull in these extra people. Most of you reading this book will be taking a big step, from one or two people responsible for youth planning, to adult team plus involvement of youth in planning. And that *is* a big step.

There is a pressing need for coordination between church school and "night group." When values clarification became the big "in" thing to do in youth groups, often the night group advisors would hear: "We've been doing that in church school for the last six weeks."

I would like to see the church school curriculum, which suggests activities for which the church school hour is too short, carried over into the "fellowship" program. For example, if we knew ahead that our junior highs were going ot be studying symbols of the Christian faith in the morning, think of the gorgeous banners and creative worship experiences which could be planned and carried out as a Worship activity on Sunday nights or on a Saturday afternoon. The product could be shared with the congregation on Sunday morning or at a special service.

If the church school teachers were on the youth ministry team, the leaders could collaborate and make suggestions for activities which would promote church school in such a way that the youth would want to be a part of both, Sunday morning and Sunday night. Some of you probably have the problem of one group of youth coming to church school and a completely different group coming to night group. We need to coordinate. We need to know what each other is doing. It certainly would beef up our Christian education program. And our church school teachers would get the extra support they need.

Scout leaders could clue the leadership team in on interests, talents, activities, and service projects of our youth. And think of the outstanding worship experiences if we got the choir and instrumental directors in on it.

Are you dreaming with me? I don't have an A-B-C plan for getting these folks on board. Once you have experienced the possibilities of an increased youth ministry through the leadership team approach, I have confidence you can work to get these other leaders involved in the next couple of years. My best advice is to get them to the planning retreat, for that is where the year is planned and where adults and youth have opportunities to get to know each other. Then, keep the channels of communication open and call full youth ministry team meetings when needed.

This expanded team would coordinate a calendar of all activities involving youth in, with, and around the church. It would also work together in one coordinated effort at publicity which would benefit all groups involved.

Youth Council/Officers

Anyone who has ever been in a workshop with me knows of my strong bias against youth councils and officers of youth groups. I realize that the young people who serve in these roles often turn out to be responsible church members, seminary students, and the like. That's great, but I want *all* our kids to have that opportunity of responsibility and leadership. There are too many churches with a sharp core group of youth, but they cannot get the rest of the kids involved.

What we create with officers and special leadership groups, like youth councils, is an "elite." Upon election or appointment, the elite take charge and everyone else lays back. They are not motivated to participate until they get a chance to be on the youth council. By choosing or electing such a group, we are also adding to the basic problem of teen-agers, their need to be accepted and to belong. Those who are not elected are left out. They are not "in," as they say, in the "in group"—at least not this year.

Kids get enough exclusions during their adolescence. The church does not need to add to this problem. Rather, the church should be going out of its way to include *all youth.* That is why this leadership team concept advocates responsible persons. Each and every one of the youth has opportunities to plan, to work personally with adult advisors, to lead, and to gather resources. We want youth to feel important and needed.

If you absolutely have to have a youth council, or are in a situation where youth councils have worked well, meaning that the other kids in your youth group are also active, then use your youth council with this leadership team approach. It is suggested in chapter 3 that youth be in on the initiation of this process. Their responses and suggestions are needed. A youth council would be the logical group with whom to begin discussion of this concept. They would be of great help in promoting and publicizing youth ministry. They would be the sounding board for ideas on setting up the team ministry.

The youth council could be of great help in planning and setting up the planning retreat. They could also attend leadership team meetings throughout the year. These youth can aid in evaluating the "program."

I would not include the youth council on the "team." I would prefer to say that all youth are on the youth ministry team or just call the adults the leadership team. Again, I am worried about exclusion. Ten to twelve adults and four youth on the team would promote the elitist feeling. I will go along with the youth council working with the leadership team, but not "being" the team. This may be nit-picking on my part, but I value so strongly the worth and acceptance of each and every young person in our churches, that I feel the need to eliminate anything that intimates exclusiveness.

So, if you do have a youth council, I recommend a downplaying of their importance and an uplifting of the importance of every individual young person in the group.

14
Moving into the Second Year

Success

Do not expect great successes the first year. Do not be surprised if attendance does not increase or if the enthusiasm of the youth is not what you expected it to be. It takes time to develop youth ministry. It takes time to build enthusiasm. Please do not throw out this approach because you did not get immediate results. The first year is usually rough. It may not work the way "the book" says it should. It takes time to smooth out the rough spots. Resist the temptation to go back to old ways (one couple as youth advisors) because you had a troublesome year.

Evaluate! Make changes. Modify the approach before discarding it after one year. Your periodic evaluation will be your guide for Year Two. You will learn through evaluation what needs to be done differently next year. You may decide to combine two categories, as suggested in chapter 13. Some of your leaders may want to switch categories or switch to the other age group.

Leadership Changes

Around March you should ask the team members to indicate by a certain date whether or not they would like to continue in youth ministry another year. If they choose to continue, ask if they would like to change categories or age groups.

Coordinators: Check with each leader, so that you will know how many will need to be recruited. Ask the present leaders to consider accompanying you on visits to potential leaders.

Leadership Training

You may need to change the way in which the leadership team was trained (see chapter 16). Our team suggested having a leadership retreat the second year, instead of the orientation cookout and four nightly training sessions. That is a great idea. However, one would need to find out if the leaders could get away for two retreats (this and the planning retreat) within a four-to-six-week period.

If you get your leaders recruited early enough, you could have a spring leadership team retreat and then have the new team in operation during the summer. Summer activities are often good opportunities for new leaders to get to know the youth. They also help in the integration of the new class of kids, those who will be in junior and senior high for the first time.

Four nights of leadership training may be a little much for the veteran leaders. But whatever you choose for the training event, encourage the old leaders to attend for the sake of team building. The new leaders will function better if they can catch the team spirit.

You may find you want to try a Saturday or Sunday workshop instead of the four nights of training. Consider bringing in a resource person, an educator who does youth ministry, for one or two of your sessions. This may encourage the old as well as the new leaders to attend.

Change of Dates

After you have completed the first year, you may find that you want to start the next year earlier. You

might train the team in May, have the planning retreat in June and start with summer programming. You could have the parent meeting in the summer or in late August. If you have regular summer youth meetings, late August may be the best time for the planning retreat. Then your calendar would begin with September.

There is no one right way to do youth ministry. Work out a schedule which seems best for your situation. Due to the different makeup of youth groups from year to year, you may need to change your schedule to suit the particular group of youth.

Expanded Youth Leadership

If you follow through with the responsible person concept, you will discover leadership qualities in your young people. This is important. It is hard for adults to turn over responsibilities to youth. Granted, many youth cannot take responsibilities without a lot of nudging. But by working with them as responsible persons in planning and by giving them a few opportunities to lead, the groundwork is laid for responsible leadership.

In setting up summer events, you can recruit responsible persons. Also, for the next planning retreat, a group of responsible persons would be beneficial.

Take advantage of opportunities to evaluate with the youth. Their feedback will give you a clearer idea of the direction youth ministry is taking and of the capabilities of various young people. Year by year, you will see your youth taking more leadership roles. See chapter 15, "Youth as Leaders."

Larger Youth Ministry Team

After the first year or so, you may be able to expand the youth ministry team to include church school teachers, scout leaders, music directors, etc. See chapter 13.

Need/Goal-Oriented Youth Ministry

I mentioned earlier that this approach is not based on assessed needs and goals of the individual youth group. Rather, it is based on the general need—for all youth to be involved in all aspects of the life of the church, which becomes the goal.

In most other youth leadership planning materials, it is suggested that you go through a process of assessing needs and establishing goals for the group. I agree that this is an important process; however, I have seen it bog down a youth group, especially one that has not been exposed to wide varieties of ministry.

After a year or two of this leadership team approach, based on involvement of youth in the five areas of the church's life, the youth should be capable of discovering the needs of their own group. Being exposed to the various aspects of ministry, they can begin to talk about meaningful goals related to their needs, the needs of the church, and their life together in the Christian community.

During this first year, the youth have been given responsibility in planning and leadership, and have participated in lots of evaluation. Thus, they should begin to comprehend the meaning of youth ministry and the meaning of the life and mission of the church. With this background, they can start talking about needs, direc-tion, and goal setting. Youth, together with adult leaders, can begin to discover the needs and plan youth ministry in light of these needs.

Youth ministry is a growing process and, as with any type of growth, has its pains, its spurts, and its dormancy. I hope this leadership team approach can be a starting point. I hope it offers to you new ways for adults and youth to work together, new ways to utilize the talents and capabilities of members of your congregation. But most of all, I hope it can be the start of a vital youth ministry, one in which your young people will feel wanted, respected, and affirmed, and one in which they can experience the Christian community by their actual participation in that community.

Section C
Building Leadership

15
Youth as Leaders

What comes to your mind when you think of "youth as leaders?" Do you picture a senior high group with fellow members up front leading the meeting or doing the program? Do you picture a junior high group with a senior high functioning in the place of adult advisors?

We often have a narrow concept of what a leader is and does. This chapter is not about phasing in youth as advisors, while phasing out adults. It is not about youth standing up in front of their group, managing all their activities and problems.

I remember one adult advisor telling me about his group which was led totally by the youth. The kids ran their own group. I thought that was fantastic, until I found out that what was actually happening was the youth were taking turns getting up a program for Sunday night. At the beginning of the year, they signed up for Sunday nights, and were responsible for the program when their turn came around. Youth group was a collection of adult speakers, who spoke on whatever subject they knew something about. Often there was no program. Either the designated young person forgot or could not find anybody. Volleyball became the program. This is not youth leadership.

Roles of Leadership

Youth leadership encompasses any actions, assignments, or roles for which youth take responsibility. There is a great variety of things youth can do in ministry which develop leadership skills. Consider the following:

Tutors
Small group leaders
Teachers of younger grades
Teachers in nursery
Teachers and helpers in vacation Bible school
Leaders of music

Teaching talents/skills to any age group
Leading activities as instructor (games, group-building activities)
Taking responsibilities in cooking, cleanup, gathering resources, setting up room, preparing materials
Worship leaders
Piano/organ/guitar accompaniment
Audio-visual resource persons
Publicity
Telephoning
Writing articles for newsletters (editor of a youth newsletter or a division of church newsletter)
Directing drama
In charge of puppet ministry (directors, set designers)
Leading sports activities for younger children
Leading children's activities during family night suppers or fellowship groups
Leading intergenerational activities
Telling stories

In most churches youth are not ready to assume many of these leadership roles. They are used to the adults doing everything for them. In this leadership team approach, the tendency could be to let the youth do nothing, since there are so many adults to do whatever is needed. The leadership team should be aware of this tendency. Coordinators and leaders constantly need to be evaluating the program to see if there are things adults are doing which could be done by youth.

Assessing Your Situation

Taking a look at your church situation will help in evaluating the participation or lack of participation by youth. Participation, motivation, and leadership by youth all go hand in hand. Where there has been low participation by youth in youth group, there is an indication of low motivation. Where there is low motivation, there is practically no leadership or responsible roles taken by youth.

Below is a continuum of youth participation, ranging from low to high youth involvement:

A   B   Ca   Cb   D   E

On it are placed six church situations. Which description fits your church?

Church A. Youth groups meet on Sunday. There are two leaders responsible for program. They alternate Sunday nights. They scrounge around to "get up a program," pulling an idea from here and there, whatever the leader can find for the kids to do.

Church B. The adult leaders do a fairly good job of organizing a Sunday night program. The success of this program depends on the luck of the church in finding a cracker-jack advisor each year. So, one year they have a good youth group, and the next year not so hot.

Church Ca. This church has a good youth group which is heading in the direction of a balanced youth program, with activities in all five areas. They use youth in planning and follow the process for planning suggested in this book. The youth are coming, but are not taking any responsibility for the group (other than at the planning retreat). In other words, the adult leaders did not follow through on the responsible persons. The group does other things together besides Sunday night.

Church Cb. This church is in the same situation as the one above, Ca, except that responsible persons are utilized which means that youth are developing leadership skills.

Church D. This church uses the youth ministry team approach. The youth are involved in all areas of the life of the church. They are active and learning leadership skills.

Church E. This church has an expanded youth ministry team. There is an effort to coordinate all that happens in the church with youth—Sunday night group, Sunday morning church school classes, youth club program, scouts, youth choir. All leaders or teachers connected in any way with youth are on the youth ministry team. The youth are involved. They care about what happens in their church. They are used to taking leadership roles.

There is a definite difference between Ca and Cb. The advisors in Ca do not carry out the responsible persons concept. If this continues year after year, that church cannot expect increased participation by the youth. Youth need to be given responsibility in order to develop ownership in their group.

Even churches at the D and E level will get bogged down if they are not developing responsibility in their youth. The responsible persons concept is crucial to this development. Otherwise, churches at D and E will continue to cry out: How do we motivate the youth to come? How do we get them to participate once they get there?

If you have not had an active youth group for five years, then you are at Point A or even further to the left, off the continuum. Your youth will not readily take active roles in leadership. They would have no inclination to do so.

If you are at the other end of the continuum, a church with a pattern of youth leadership already established, then you will see youth taking more and more responsibility in leadership roles as your "program" increases.

I have included this continuum to give those of you in A and B situations some reassurance. If you are starting out on this leadership team approach, you could easily get discouraged. Your youth are used to adults taking care of the program. Adults have always carried the responsibility for all the activities. The youth are used to just "coming to youth group."

I doubt if you will be seeing any miracles this year just because you have a new approach to youth ministry, no matter how hard you work at it. Youth cannot move from A (adult-centered youth program) to E (voluntary, enthusiastic, responsible participation) in one year. You cannot expect initiative on the young people's part. They are not used to it. What is needed to develop leadership and responsibility among the youth is time, patience, sensitivity, and a lot of adult support.

Developing Leadership and Responsibility

Developing leadership does not mean turning the youth program over to the kids. That would be like trying to jump from A to E. In fact, turning the program over to the kids should not be the goal. That would indicate a misunderstanding of youth leadership. Keep in mind the variety of leadership roles suggested on page 98. There are so many responsibilities youth can learn to handle.

Our goal is to give each individual young person the kind of responsibilities he or she can handle, and to equip him or her with the leadership skills to assume even greater responsibilities. Through the process of trying out leadership roles, the youth will gradually gain ownership of their youth program. They no longer will

just "go to youth group." They will be motivated to go because they planned it, helped get projects together, publicized it, and made phone calls. They care about whether a particular activity is a success or failure because they have an investment in it.

Likewise, their interest and participation in the life of their church should gradually increase as they begin to take leadership responsibilities in other areas of the church's life.

Now that we know where we are headed, how are we going to get there? How do we develop leadership skills in our youth?

Responsible Persons

The responsible persons concept, which is an essential part of youth ministry as described in this book, is a starting place. Every young person has the opportunity to plan the activities that make up the year's program. Each of the youth will work closely with an adult leader. Here the youth are exposed to all the responsibilities that go into developing these activities. Depending on their abilities and interests, the youth can take any number of responsibilities related to the activities—getting resources, shopping, setting up the room, leading an exercise, monitoring a small group, phoning, publicizing. In this process the youth learn through experience. The more responsibilities they take, the more confidence they develop.

The adult leader plays an important role in developing leadership skills. The adult leaders are the models of leadership. The responsible persons, through observing the adults as well as through working with those adults, will pick up clues as to how responsibilities are carried out. Through planning with the adults, the youth are brought in on all that goes into developing an activity, project, or event. They should learn quite a bit.

The adult also becomes the support so crucially needed for young people to be willing to try on that new responsible role.

A Few Tips for Leaders

Coordinators: Pass this information on to your leaders as they prepare to work with their responsible persons.

Sensitivity

It will take a great amount of sensitivity for the leaders to figure out who is ready for a particular leadership task and how much responsibility that individual can handle. The relationship between youth and adult is so important. As the adult leader gets to know the young person better, the adult will be able to discern what tasks to suggest. Because of a trusting relationship, the young person is freer to accept responsibilities which may be beyond what that youth would normally do. Growth is taking place.

Clarity of Expectations

The youth need to know exactly what they are expected to do in a certain task. Give them the specifics —a list of what they need to do, how they might go about it, by what date it needs to be done, and who to call if they have any questions or need help.

Support—Side by Side

Some youth will need to perform the responsible task right alongside the adult. In fact, in some situations the adult leader will do the task with the young person serving as a sidekick. Other youth will be able to tackle the job as long as the leader is there. And still other youth will be ready to make a go of it alone. Leaders need to be sensitive to know which of the youth can go it alone and which need the side by side support. The difficulty of the task makes a difference. A young person who has taken responsibilities in phoning and resourcing may be ready to try leading a group through a series of values exercises, but may wish to have the adult leader there, just in case.

Support—in Times of Failure

One of the risks in taking on any leadership role is that of failure. Now all you adults should be getting a little seasoned in this area. You may already know what it is like to look foolish because something bombed. Or, at least, you no doubt have had a few butterflies over one of your activities failing. If so, your aching experience is paying off. You are in a good position to empathize, for these young people will shake through many of their new leadership responsibilities, especially if the role involves getting up in front of a group.

Failure is not bad. It is true that we learn from our mistakes, but there is more value to failure than that. Failure brings out the strong qualities of a relationship. Going through failure of any kind with a young person will enhance your relationship with that young person. In failure we need each other, because it hurts. One caution: Do not minimize the situation. What looks totally harmless can be devastating to a young person. Be there. Be supportive. Let the kid know you hurt with him or her. Let the kid talk it out. And after a while you will both find healing and can "get on with it."

Failure often has the same effect on a youth group. I bombed miserably with a program I was leading once. When I brought it to a halt and admitted it was a disaster, I could feel within the group a mass of support.

Let's not underestimate kids. Cruel and cliquish as they can be, they are capable of some of the most caring and loving responses.

Support—in Times of Success

Every once-in-awhile, when a group of kids does something terrific, I'll catch myself going over to a couple of adult leaders and praising the kids for what they did, neglecting to say anything to the kids themselves. Tragic error! These kids need affirmation. We should affirm them whenever possible. Once you have given a responsibility, recognize the youth at the completion of the task. You don't need a ceremony; simply tell them what a good job they did.

Recognize the efforts of various individuals. Let the congregation know which youth are doing what. Periodically arrange for the congregation to express its appreciation for the involvement of the youth in the total church program.

Youth Taking Adult Roles

There will be times when the youth can assume a leadership role normally taken by an adult. In these cases, all that is said above needs to be doubled. They will need extra support and extra training. Tasks should be very clearly stated.

If it is a situation where the youth will be serving on a committee or task force with a group of adults, I highly recommend having a workshop on youth ministry for those adults. So often when youth serve on an adult committee, the adults either ignore them or ask questions that are not as important as those asked of adult members. Adults on committees need skills in relating to young people.

Give Them Leadership Opportunities

After all this talk about how to develop leadership, it seems ridiculous to have to say: Do give them leadership opportunities. But it does need to be said, and repeated. There is a danger in this leadership team approach of leaders doing everything themselves, because they can do it quicker than enlisting the youth. Leaders will forget to call responsible persons. They run out of time, plan the activity themselves, and never give the youth a chance to be responsible. I have made this mistake. So have several of our adult leaders. You just get too busy.

Therefore, the very first step in developing leadership skills in youth is to take seriously the responsible persons. Call them together. Discuss leadership possibilities and responsibilities. And then do give the youth the opportunities. It is less trouble to do it all yourself, but then the youth will never be able to make an investment in their own program. And as their motivation to take ownership disappears, so does their enthusiasm and participation.

Youth Ministry: The New Team Approach

16
Leadership Training Sessions

I wish that there were one book that would tell potential youth leaders all they would need to know about youth, the church, youth ministry, and skills for working with youth. Even if there were one book, it would be wishful thinking to expect every leader to read it.

There is no way I can convey in one chapter all that one should do as training for the leadership team, which usually takes three or four sessions. However, most of what has been written in the chapters of this book has been used in the training of adult leadership teams.

If you can, bring in an outside resource person to deal with the general information youth leaders need to have: age group characteristics, youth and their culture, how to relate to youth, skills and methods needed for doing youth ministry. As to the specifics of the leadership team approach, all the leaders need to know is in this book, especially in chapters 1, 2, 5, 10, and 11.

Coordinators: Since it is your job to set up the training sessions, you will need to be very familiar with this book. In this chapter I will outline a set of leadership training sessions, a structure that may help you in designing the training. As nice as it would be to just have everybody read this book and ask questions, I need to remind you that *the purpose of the leadership sessions is not just training, but team building as well.* Structured into these sessions are opportunities for team members to get to know each other and to experience working together.

At the orientation, described in chapter 7, the leaders had an opportunity to discuss and ask questions about this youth ministry team approach. Therefore, we can assume that the basic concepts have been covered.

However, there still may be plenty of questions and dilemmas to work out. The concept of a balanced youth program, using the five categories, was introduced at the youth cookout and may have been used at the Parent Night. Thus, most leaders should be familiar with the use of the five category, balanced program.

The following is a list of what I see as the major areas needing attention at the training sessions:

1. Team-building activities
2. The purpose of youth ministry
   —what do we want for youth today? what are our dreams, goals, expectations?
   —a theological frame of reference
3. Who they (youth) are
   —characteristics of this age group
   —needs of this age
   —the world they live in—their culture, school, interests
   —what kids are like today—what's different about today's kids
4. Who you are, the adult leader
   —how to relate to youth
   —what kind of relationship is possible
   —problems in relating
   —leadership styles
   —responsibilities as a member of the leadership team
5. Planning with youth
   —the planning retreat
   —how responsible persons function
   —how this process motivates active participation by youth
6. Relating to parents
   —enlisting their support
   —ways to involve parents
   —Parent Night

7. Interpreting youth ministry to the congregation
   —communication, publicity
   —visibility of the youth
   —brainstorming ways to interpret
8. Resources
9. Dilemmas

It is difficult to write out a four-session leadership training design and offer it to you. No two youth ministry workshops I have done have ever been alike. The best advice I can offer is to encourage you to study the list of nine items above and design your own training.

One of my problems is I never know where to start. Should I plow into the responsibilities of leaders first thing, since that is a pressing need of leaders who attend? A proper place to start seems to be "purpose of youth ministry," but if it is too "lecture-y," I would worry about losing them to boredom. Characteristics of youth seems to be another logical starting place.

I really don't think it matters where you start. Keep in mind two things: (1) Pacing—a little lecture/explanation followed by a group builder or a move into small groups. Don't let one session drag so badly that they won't want to come back. (2) The needs of the group—coordinators should be getting a feel for what the leaders need most. Don't spend time on characteris-

tics of the age group, if most of the leaders have read up on youth or seem to be in tune with youth today.

I usually begin a workshop by asking the group what they want to get out of the workshop; what their expectations and needs are. I write down everything they say and arrange my agenda accordingly. Of course, they do get a few items they didn't ask for. For example, a group may not suggest "how to relate to parents." But, because parent support is crucial to youth ministry, I include it anyway.

If you have access to a resource person, an educator with a specialty in youth ministry, go over the nine items with him or her. That resource person may want to speak to three or four issues. You can arrange to do those three in one session.

The following is a sample outline, drawn from the list of nine items. It is just a sample. Rearrange it to suit your situation. Make sure to write out the four-session agenda on newsprint, so that the leaders can see where you are going. They can add questions and concerns they perceive won't be covered.

In this example, the leaders have already had an orientation session. They know the basics and the rationale of this approach. They have already used the five category form (see p. 41). The youth and leaders filled these out at the youth cookout.

Youth Ministry: The New Team Approach

One of the most important ingredients in a workshop or a leadership education class is the sharing of ideas, the learning that comes not from what the teacher says, but from the suggestions and experiences of the other participants.

Coordinators: Your leaders need to be told this. I have seen situations where class participants took notes only when the teacher was speaking. Tell the team that they will learn a great deal from each other and, therefore, should be alert to the contributions of all participants.

These sessions take about an hour and a half each. Numbers in parentheses refer to numbers of resources listed in chapter 17.

SESSION I

Agenda: Who they are—youth
Who you are in relation to them
Your expectations—what you would like to
see happen with youth today

In preparation for this session, the leader and participants should read chapter 8 of this book and, if possible, any of the following:

—chapters 2 and 3 of *The Exuberant Years* (#3)
—chapter 1 of *Youth—A Manual for CE:SA* (#2)
—sections I and II of *PYM Youth Manual* (#1)
—chapters 4 and 5 of *Creative Youth Leadership* (#4)

1. Team Builder (Four Facts/One Lie)

This group builder could be used as the initial activity or used in the middle of the session, after a break. (See Appendix C, no. 20.) You could use the following statements:

The furthest I have ever been from home . . .
The oddest job I ever had . . .
The most daring (either risky or stupid) thing I
ever did . . .
My favorite song . . .

2. Who They Are

Draw a line down the middle of a sheet of newsprint. Across the top write:

What I like about youth	What I don't like about youth

Give the group five to ten minutes to brainstorm, listing characteristics they like about teen-agers and those they don't like. Some items will overlap.

Discuss the characteristics. Note those that group members came across in readings.

Ask the group to point out which are more characteristic of junior highs, and which of senior highs.

3. Needs of Youth

On a newsprint sheet, write the following:

Needs of Youth

—to be liked

—to be loved

—space (to develop independence)

—attention

—to be important, respected (a sense of worth)

—to belong

—to be understood

Discuss these needs. The group may wish to add to the list.

4. Who You Are in Relation to Them

Break into small groups of three.

The task is to come up with a description of a leader of youth. Take into consideration the needs of youth previously discussed. Describe the kind of relationship the leader would have with youth. What qualities and characteristics would he or she have? Appoint a recorder/reporter. Each group is to come up with one composite description.

After fifteen minutes, bring everyone together. Have the reporter from each group read the descriptions. Ask everyone: What is realistic about this leader? What is unrealistic?

Go on to the next group.

5. Our Expectations

Ask participants to think for a minute about what they would like to see happen with the youth in their church. This is an opportunity to dream of ideal youth ministries. What do you want for youth today? List everyone's contribution on newsprint.

The following expectations came out of a workshop of youth advisors and church school teachers. Do not use this list. It is merely to give you an idea of the kinds of expectations youth leaders have.

— to be challenged to grow beyond themselves (theologically, socially, relationally)
— to be caring for others, church, Jesus Christ
— to learn the faith (in a meaningful way)
— to grapple with the faith and what it means to them

— to gain basic Bible knowledge
— to know what makes them Presbyterian (or other denomination), their tradition
— to have Christian friends
— to be proud to be Christians
— to know the joy of salvation (grace)
— to have commitment to the church as an alternative to culture/consumerism
— to have identity as a church member
— to be able to defend their position as Christians when faced with cults, etc.
— to reach out and want to reach out beyond their group, to bring other youth in
— to be articulate in their faith
— to be able to doubt, question
— to be responsible and to respect other human beings
— to feel accepted
— to gain exposure to problems in world beyond what they normally deal with
— to be honest
— to make decisions

For Next Session

a) Have the group see what they can find out about youth culture today. What is a teen-ager's world like in 19__? What do they do? What influences affect them? What is school like? What about relationships to friends? to parents? to authority figures?

b) Those who have access to this book should read chapter 2 in preparation for a discussion on the purpose of youth ministry.

SESSION II

Agenda: The world of today's youth
The purpose of youth ministry
Interpreting youth ministry to the congregation
Responsibilities of the leaders

1. Team Builder

Have the following unfinished sentences written on newsprint or on a chalkboard before leaders arrive:

When I was a teen-ager, an embarrassing thing that happened to me was . . .
A time my parents made me angry was . . .
During my youth, a time when I was on top of the world was . . .

Pass out paper and pencils. Instruct everyone to write down an answer, a completion to each of the sentences.

After everyone has finished, divide the group into small groups of three. They are to share their completions for the first sentence with the others in the group. Then go on to the second sentence, then the third.

2. World of Today's Youth

On a chalkboard or a piece of newsprint turned sideways make the following columns:

school	other places they go	relationship to parents	friends	relationship to church	interests	influences

Let the group discuss their findings and their impressions of youth today. Jot down information in each column. The group may add other headings.

When they have finished, ask if there is anything you left out. Is this a picture of youth today?

3. Purpose of Youth Ministry

During this time a summary could be made of chapter 2. The following are statements of the main points found in that chapter.

Youth Ministry: A Theological Frame of Reference

Youth ministry cannot exist apart from the church.

The goal of youth ministry is the same as that of the church—that all members be involved in the total life of the congregation, which includes its worship, study, ministry within the congregation, service, and fellowship.

Youth are members of the community of faith, the church, *now.* They are not future members.

The church is founded on Jesus Christ and is commissioned to proclaim God's goodness, power, and love.

The purpose of the church is to take up the difficult and glorious struggle of knowing and doing the will of God as a community of faith. Youth are involved in this struggle.

The community of faith is the teacher of the young. Youth learn about the Christian faith by participating in the life of the church, not just by the church school.

The community of faith is a community of change and challenge. The challenge for the church today is to participate in the transformation of the world on behalf of the good news of Jesus Christ.

Youth ministry is necessary so that the church can:
—respond to the specific needs of youth;
—support its young people;
—offer a context and a place in which youth can get together with their peers;
—offer youth opportunities to explore, question, and grow through various stages of commitment.

What we are about in youth ministry and in the church is a commitment to a *Person,* Jesus Christ, over and above a commitment to a cause, a belief, a theology, a value system, or a lifestyle.

Questions for discussion:
—*What ideas about the purpose of youth ministry are new to you?*

—*Do you think our church is willing to treat young people as full members of the congregation? If not, why not?*
—*How do you respond to the idea that the church school is not the main vehicle through which we learn about the Christian faith?*

4. Interpreting Youth Ministry to the Congregation

Explain to the team the problem of communicating to the congregation what is going on in youth ministry, both through publicity and through interpretation of the purpose of youth ministry.

Ask the group to think of ways to communicate and interpret. Brainstorm. List all ideas on newsprint. (See chapter 12 for additional ideas.)

Pick two or three to work on. Discuss ways of implementing the ideas. Who should be responsible? How can we involve youth in the effort? When should we get started?

5. Responsibilities of the Leaders

Now is the time to make sure all leaders understand what their responsibilities are. Use chapter 5, the "Leaders' Chapter" as a guideline. Mimeograph the following page for the leaders. Go over the responsibilities as listed.

SESSION III

Agenda: Leadership styles
Involving parents
Resources and methods

1. Leadership Styles

Before the session copy the five styles on five pieces of newsprint, one on each piece. Put these up on the wall in five different parts of the room.

This exercise is designed to give leaders an opportunity to consider what they would do as leaders in various problem situations. It encourages them to identify their responses to these situations with particular

RESPONSIBILITIES OF
YOUTH MINISTRY TEAM LEADERS

WITH YOUTH:

1. To build relationships (Your relationship with the youth is more important than "program.")

    a. Spend time getting to know the youth individually.
       — Start at the cookout and retreat.
       — Be there occasionally when you are not "leading." (Coordinator will call you periodically.)
       — Let them know you.

    b. Be conscioius of relationship building within the group.
       — Use group-building activities.
       — Break into small groups whenever appropriate.

2. To plan and carry out the activities in your category.

    a. Explore the possibilities for activities within your category (see Appendix B). Work at this with your category partner.

    b. List a few ideas on newsprint for the planning retreat.

    c. *Be at the planning retreat.*

    d. Be at the follow-up meeting.

    e. Keep up with the calendar. Plan ahead.

    f. *Work with the responsible persons.*
       — Call them a month ahead of an activity to meet (i.e., 20 minutes after a Sunday night meeting).
       — Give responsible persons responsibilities in gathering materials, setting up, cleaning up, sharing leadership. (Call them to remind them of their responsibilities.)

    g. At the activity, event, project, etc.:
       — Get the needed resources and materials.
       — Be there early.
       — Facilitate interaction within the group. (Try to draw out those who have not contributed. Don't let one person dominate.)

3. To evaluate—with your category partner, with the *responsible persons*, with the youth.

WITH YOUTH MINISTRY TEAM:

1. To be a youth advocate. Speak out for youth concerns as well as for youth ministry.

2. To participate in team meetings. The team needs your ideas, suggestions, your evaluation.

3. To be willing to get involved right at the start.

4. To call on each other for help.

What you can expect from the church: support, resources, training, publicity leadership styles. The styles range from highly authoritarian to complete absence of adult leadership.

Identifying one's style of leadership can be helpful in understanding how one relates to young people. What usually emerges from this exercise is that a leader cannot pigeonhole himself or herself as one particular style. We all have elements of the many styles within us. We respond differently to different situations. This is good. It is unlikely that any of us could adopt a certain style and respond to every situation consistently out of that style.

The following are the five styles we will consider. These are not all-inclusive. There could be variations on each of the five. Try to work with the five described here:

The Ultimate Authority: Takes charge. Makes all decisions for the welfare of the group. Tells them what the rules are. Youth have no say in matters. Dictates the solution to a problem. Plans the program.

Chief: Determines the direction the group will take. Suggests programs/solutions to the group. The youth get to discuss programs/solutions, but the leader has control over which solution will be carried out. Leader is the program planner.

Consulter: Determines the structure or limits within which the group will function. Allows decisions to be made by the group, except in matters where the adult knows best. Leader does consult the group before making any decision. Gets their feelings and ideas.

Democratizer: Youth determine the structure. Youth come up with alternatives of program or possible solutions to a problem. The democratizer lets youth rule by consensus in all matters. This leader guides youth in examining alternatives, helping them to see consequences, but does not sway them to a particular solution.

Hands Offist: Waits and sees what happens—in a given situation. Youth make all decisions, solve their own problems in whatever way they choose. They create their own youth program. They determine their own leadership among themselves.

Explain that there are five possible styles of leadership posted around the room. Read each, then tell the group that you are going to give them a situation. They are to decide what they would actually do in that situation. Once they have decided, then they are to determine in which leadership style category that decision would fall.

Below are listed five situations. You will probably have time for three.

#1 You are in the middle of a mini-course on values, which is designed to help youth learn how to make decisions about their own values and their life goals. One of your regular attenders says to you at supper: "We're not going to do any more of that values stuff, are we? We're getting tired of it. We did that last year."

What would you do?

#2 You are getting the idea that there is a lot of hostility in the group. There seem to be two groups at war with each other. You find out that one of these groups led a campaign to prevent a girl (also a member of your group) from becoming a cheerleader—and succeeded! And now hostility is destroying the group.

What would you do?

#3 In the middle of a contemporary worship service, which your youth have created, prepared, and are leading, a girl stands up and says: "This worship service is a real bummer. It's deadly. Worship is a joyful experience. We should be shouting, dancing, and singing praise to God."

What would you do?

#4 Three kids in your group have come up to you at different times, begging to bring friends to the September 23-24 planning retreat. You asked if these friends plan to attend your group regularly. The answer was no all three times. These friends are active in their own church youth groups.

What would you do?

#5 You are in the bunk bed at a retreat. It is 2:00 A.M. You overhear two youth talking about two other kids who have brought alcohol on the retreat. The two youth who are talking think you are asleep.

What would you do?

After determining which style of leadership your decision comes under, go to the part of the room where that style is posted and discuss solutions with others who have chosen the same style. Ask that each group have one person report on the group's discussion. After each group has reported, go on to the next situation.

Not only does this exercise help leaders discover that they have aspects of all five styles, but it also gives them a chance to discuss actual problems that could and do arise in youth groups.

2. Team Builder

Divide the group into the two teams—all junior high leaders in one group, all senior high leaders in the

other. Coordinators meet with their respective groups. Have everyone think about how to complete this sentence:

> What worries me about working on the youth ministry team is . . .

Go around the circle, letting each person complete the statement.

Coordinators: Listen carefully. Make a few notes. Some leaders may have similar worries. Now is the time to discuss some of these worries. Clear up misinformation. Encourage the group to help each other find ways to alleviate the worries. This is the supportive part of working as a team.

3. Involving Parents

Parent support and involvement is essential to an active youth ministry program. As is discussed in chapter 9, parents can be either a great asset or one of your main problems. Parents need to understand what their youth are involved in at church. And they need an opportunity to be a part of it.

Begin this section by discussing ways parents have been involved in the past as well as problems the church may have had with lack of parent support.

On a clean sheet of newsprint, let the group brainstorm all the possible ways parents could be involved. This list should include ways parents can be of help as well as ideas for activities which involve parents and youth together. (See chapter 9 for suggestions.)

After listing all ideas, consider implementing some of these suggestions. These ideas could be incorporated into your Parent Night. Also, the leaders should make note of ideas for activities which fall into their categories. Plan to discuss these activities with the youth at the planning retreat.

4. Resources and Methods

Lay out on tables the youth ministry resources you have.

Coordinators: You need to be familiar with a good portion of these if you are to be of help to the leaders. Give the group ample time (20-30 minutes) to browse through the materials.

There are two things to look for in programmatic materials:

a) Ideas — Most of the materials will hit on many of the topics, issues, concerns, and activities that leaders have already been considering for their categories. In the materials they will find a variety of ways to approach these areas.

b) Methods — The average leader may think that the only method to use with youth is discussion. By browsing through programmatic materials, they will find various methods and activities to use in dealing with a specific topic. Encourage the leaders to sign out one of these books to examine more closely. (See chapter 17, nos. 3, 22–44.)

You should also have several youth leaders' guides available. The following have sections on methods:

The Exuberant Years, chapter 6 (#3)
Youth—A Manual for Christian Education: Shared Approaches, chapter 2 (#2)
Creative Youth Leadership, chapter 8 (#4)

Point out these chapters. Chapter 17, the resource list, may be of help to you in buying or borrowing resources.

The best way to learn a method is to *do* it. Reading about methods or hearing someone describe them does not give leaders the confidence they need to use them with youth.

Point out the variety of methods used in the training sessions:

> brainstorming
> categorizing
> sentence completions
> discussion
> small group work
> browsing
> research (on background
>   reading)
> group builders
> handouts
> short lecture (talk)

If You Have Time

If you have time, you could do the following Bible study activity. Making study of the Bible exciting, or merely interesting, to youth is a major concern of youth leaders and teachers. The following is an example of a method used in creative Bible study.

Divide into small groups of four or five each. Each group will need at least one Bible, paper, and pencils. Have one person in each group read the parable of the Good Samaritan (Luke 10:25–37). Give the following tasks:

Group 1 — Rewrite the passage in a modern-day setting.
Group 2 — Write it as a newspaper story.
Group 3 — Write it as a television interview.
Group 4 — Dramatize it.

Other options:

— Write it for second-graders, in their level of language
— Write a continuation of the story—what happened next?
— Write a different ending for it.
— Write a simple paraphrase (write it in your words).

Let each group present their interpretation.

SESSION IV

Agenda: Planning (planning retreat)
Leaders make their newsprint sheets for
  the retreat
Resources (continued)
Dilemmas

1. Planning and the Planning Retreat

Before the session mimeograph copies of the schedule for the retreat.

This is a good time to go over the schedule for the retreat. The leaders need to know what they can expect. Walk through the details of the planning process. Clarify the role of the leaders (see chapter 10).

Talk over the rules and guidelines established by the campsite, as well as those that your group will follow. Clarify with leaders their role as far as "enforcing rules" is concerned (see p. 78).

Have the leaders prepare their category sheets. Give each pair of category partners a sheet of newsprint. Have them print the category across the top. Then they are to list the three or four ideas they have chosen. Refer leaders to the list of ideas under their categories in Appendix B.

2. Resources (continued)

Have the resource materials out on tables during this session. Encourage the leaders to browse, as in the last session.

3. Dilemmas

Give the leaders an opportunity to ask questions. You may want to list the concerns they have (brainstorm) before discussing them.

Ask if there is anything they feel was not covered in the training sessions.

Encourage your leaders to try to attend all the sessions. Even leaders who have had experience and/or training in youth ministry should be there to get to know the other team members. If they cannot attend all, suggest three out of four. Any less and they would miss out on the "building of the team."

You don't have to have four sessions. And they don't have to be an hour and a half in length. Work out what is feasible in your situation. Juggle the outline. Design your own training.

Get feedback from the leaders after you have finished the leadership training. They can give you suggestions on how to do it better next year.

17
Youth Ministry Resources

Note: All prices are subject to change without notice.

GENERAL

1. *Presbyterian Youth Ministries: Youth Manual,* compiled by Jill Senior, edited by William R. Forbes, (PCUS Division of National Mission, General Assembly Mission Board, 1979), 95 pages, $5.00.

Excellent sections on characteristics of youth at each age level and the relationship between youth and adult leaders. Also sections on models, planning, and resources. The format is loose leaf, so that materials can be added. Supplementary packets for the manual will be available periodically.

2. *Youth—A Manual for Christian Education: Shared Approaches,* by David Ng (Philadelphia: Geneva Press, 1977), 48 pages, $2.25.

An essential resource for teachers of junior and senior highs. Good section on methods. Includes helps for session planning. Concise. A lot of material in 48 pages.

3. *The Exuberant Years: A Guide for Junior High Leaders,* by Ginny Ward Holderness (Atlanta: John Knox Press, 1976), 215 pages, $4.95.

Book of basics for youth leaders. Takes leader through step by step process of preparing for, planning, and developing a complete youth program. The planning process, based on involvement of youth in the total life of the church, and 11 mini-courses apply to senior highs as well.

4. *Creative Youth Leadership,* by Jan Corbett (Valley Forge, PA: Judson Press, 1977), 128 pages, $3.95.

Well done book covering all aspects of youth ministry. Includes characteristics of youth, understanding groups, methods, resources, teaching and planning skills.

5. *Youth Ministry in the Small Church* (PCUS Division of National Mission, General Assembly Mission Board, 1976), 39 pages, $1.95.

Excellent help for the small church in understanding the concept of youth ministry in the smaller church. Includes planning and specific program ideas.

6. *Resources for Youth Ministry,* edited by Michael Warren (New York: Paulist Press, 1978), 244 pages, $6.95.

An excellent collection of articles from authors experienced in youth ministry. It is directed toward Catholic parishes, but has very helpful information on developing leadership, assessing needs and designing program and evangelism. There are three chapters on Young Life. Other chapters include: Career Counseling, Ministry to Hispano Mexicano/Chicano Youth, and Adolescent Identity in Secondary Education.

7. *Youth Ministry: Sunday, Monday, and Every Day,* by John L. Carroll and Keith L. Ignatius (Judson Press, 1972), 62 pages, $1.75.

Simple, complete organization manual. Includes philosophy, needs, resources, finding and training leaders, evaluation, planning.

8. *The Complete Youth Ministries Handbook: Volume One,* edited by J. David Stone (1979), 244 pages, $10.95. Order from Creative Youth Ministry Models, Flournoy Lucas Rd., RR 2, Box 515, Shreveport, LA 71129.

A collection of chapters written by persons with experience in special aspects of youth ministry. Chapters cover: youth ministry today, models, leadership, experiential Bible study, spiritual disciplines, counseling with youth, a relational model, parents, recreation, rural ministry, clown ministry (by Bill Peckham), and a chapter on junior highs (which I wrote).

9. *Junior High Ministry: A Guidebook for the Leading and Teaching of Early Adolescents,* by Wayne Rice (Grand Rapids: Zondervan, 1978), 201 pages, $4.95.

This book goes into great detail on the development of early adolescents, including a chapter each on the following aspects of development: physical, social, mental, emotional, and spiritual.

10. *Communicating with Junior Highs,* by Robert L. Browning (Nashville: Graded Press, 1968), 208 pages.

Though this book is out of print it is still one of the best resources in ministry with junior highs. Includes description of the age group, the leaders, how to communicate with junior highs, and an excellent section on communicating the gospel.

11. *Adolescent Development and the Life Tasks,* by Guy J. Manaster (Boston: Allyn & Bacon, 1977), 337 pages, $15.95.

An in-depth textbook on adolescence. This expensive volume is recommended for leaders who would like to study all aspects of adolescent development.

12. *Young Girls: A Portrait of Adolescence,* by Gisela Konopka (Englewood Cliffs, NJ: Prentice-Hall, 1976), 176 pages, $2.95 pb ($3.25 in Canada).

Though written about girls, this excellent study, a result of hundreds of interviews, offers unique insights into the values, feelings, and thoughts of today's youth in regard to family, school, life goals, loneliness, drugs and alcohol, sexuality, and political-social concerns.

13. *Leaders Manual for Grades 6/7/8,* by Ginny Ward Holderness (Geneva Press, 1978), 94 pages, $2.10.

This manual is specifically for the church school teacher of junior highs. The planning process used in the leadership team approach is adapted in this manual to the classroom situation. Includes methods to use in the classroom, and a chapter on younger adolescents and the Bible.

14. *Teaching Early Adolescents Creatively: A Manual for Church School Teachers,* by Edward D. Seely (Philadelphia: Westminster Press, 1971), 222 pages, $2.95.

Comprehensive resource on the teaching of younger adolescents. Includes section on characteristics of this age group, resources for preparation, detailed chapters on methods, and suggestions for evaluation.

15. *New Covenant Community: A Model for Ministry with Youth in the UPCUSA* (Geneva Press, 1977), 81 pages, $2.25.

This is the product of several years of consultations and task groups seeking structure and models for youth group in the UPCUSA. The description and guidelines of *The Fellowship of the Carpenter* are found within. Includes rituals, service of commitment, symbols. The prime emphasis of this model is on group identity. I see a danger of groups becoming exclusive. But this is a model which takes commitment seriously.

16. *77 Ways of Involving Youth in the Church,* by Richard Bimler (St. Louis: Concordia, 1976), 64 pages, $3.95.

Examines all aspects of youth ministry. Touches on the role of the adult leader, barriers to youth ministry, ideas to involve youth, designs to try. Includes two adult-youth dialogues, and a variety of questionnaires to use in developing youth ministry.

17. *Will Our Children Have Faith?* by John H. Westerhoff, III (Seabury Press, 1976), 126 pages, $6.95.

I highly recommended this book in chapter 2. Westerhoff has an understanding of theology and education which our churches need. This book proposes an alternative framework for evaluating, planning, and engaging in education in the church. The life in the community of faith is the teacher of our youth. Excellent development of this theory.

18. *Youth, World, and Church,* by Sara Little (John Knox Press, 1968), 201 pages, $2.75.

A classic in youth ministry. Solid understanding of youth ministry as youth involved in mission wherever they are—church, school, home, community. Includes sections on equipping youth for mission, and the adult as servant-leader. Includes insights from various designs of youth ministry.

19. *Retreat Handbook: A Way to Meaning,* by Virgil and Lynn Nelson (Judson Press, 1976), 127 pages, $5.95.

Excellent guide to retreat planning from goal setting to organizing, getting there and following through. Guidelines and suggestions for all kinds of retreats.

20. *Guide for Recreation Leaders,* by Glenn Bannerman and Robert Fakkema (John Knox Press, 1975), 128 pages, $3.95.

Great recreation resources. Includes philosophy of recreation and play theory and many tried and true activities for all ages, for a variety of occasions, settings, and groups. Includes special section on fun for the handicapped.

21. *The New Games Book: Play Hard, Play Fair, Nobody Hurt,* edited by Andrew Fluegelman (New York: Doubleday, 1976), 194 pages, $4.95.

Excellent new games. Great for recreation, group building, simulations. Minimizes the competition.

22. *Idealog: Creative Ideas for Younger Youth,* compiled by Donald B. Schroeder, edited by William R. Forbes (Youth Elect Series, Living the Word, CE:SA, 1979), 96 pages, $4.95.

Excellent ideas for resourcing youth ministry. See guide in Appendix D.

23. *Idealog: Creative Ideas for Older Youth,* compiled by Max Haskett, edited by Guin Tuckett (YES, Living the Word, CE:SA, 1979), 96 pages, $4.95.

See guide in Appendix D.

24. *Strategies for Youth Programs: Junior High/Volume 1, 2,* edited by Barbara A. Withers (Geneva Press, 1978, 1979), 192 pages, $3.95.

In addition to excellent ideas, these volumes include articles on relating to young adolescents, developing leadership in youth, planning and leading creative worship, using games with junior highs, retreats. See Appendix D.

25. *Strategies for Youth Programs: Senior High/Volume 1,* edited by Judy R. Fletcher (Geneva Press, 1978); *Volume 2,* edited by Bernie C. Dunphy-Linnartz (1979), 192 pages, $3.95.

Includes articles on planning, leadership roles in youth ministry, and prayer. See guide, Appendix D.

26. *Youth Worker's Success Manual,* by Shirley E. Pollock (Nashville: Abingdon Press, 1978), 80 pages, $3.95.

Lots of ideas and activities in group dynamics, drama, interpersonal sensitivity, audio-visuals, service to others, worship projects, and fellowship. Appendix on how to advertise and build bulletin boards.

27. *Explore: Resources for Junior Highs in the Church,* edited by Janice M. Corbett (Judson Press, 1974), 142 pages, $5.95.

All three of the *Explore* volumes are excellent. In this, the first, is a good section on helps for leaders. Resources for designing four-to-seven-session units on: Friendship, Identity, Values/Beliefs, Social Issues, the Arts. Includes worship resources.

28. *Explore: Volume 2,* edited by James E. Grant (Judson Press, 1976), 144 pages, $5.95.

Resources for group study, retreats, projects, exercises, art experiences on the subjects of: Faith, Communication, Inner Struggles, Pop Culture, Building Community. Includes worship, leadership, and recreation resources.

29. *Explore: Volume 3,* edited by Barbara Middleton (Judson Press, 1978), 128 pages, $5.95.

Resources for sessions on: Faith, Feelings, Relationships, Decisions, Lifestyle. Includes additional program ideas and leadership helps, including an excellent three-page statement on the theological basis for youth ministry.

30. *Respond: A Resource Book for Youth Ministry, Volume 1,* edited by Keith Ignatius (Judson Press, 1971), 142 pages, $4.95.

Programmatic resources. Designed for use in youth groups or retreats. Topics: Communication, Exploring the Word of God, Issues in Your Town. Includes several hymns and songs, resources for youth and leaders, ideas for planning and evaluating, and suggestions for retreats.

31. *Respond: Volume 2,* edited by Jan Corbett (Judson Press, 1972), 143 pages, $4.95.

Resources built around issues and ideas, such as: The Church, Ecology, Meditation, Politics, Race Relations, Eastern Religions, International Mission, Easter, Sexuality. Included is a special section for junior high programs. Also, celebration resources, a simulation, and helps for adult leaders.

32. *Respond: Volume 3,* edited by Mason L. Brown (Judson Press, 1973), 140 pages, $4.95.

More resources and program ideas concerning relevant issues: Exploring the Word of God, Ecology, Evangelism, Christian Faith, Meditation, Meeting Personal Needs, the Christian and the Community, Sexuality, Vocation, Literature and Faith. Sections on celebration, camping, fund raising, mission, the occult.

33. *Respond: Volume 4,* edited by Barbara Middleton (Judson Press, 1975), 142 pages, $5.95.

Resources for study on: Bible, Christian Faith, the Christian Community, the Church, Ecology, Evangelism, Group Development, Leisure, Personal Development, Political Involvement, Relationships, Vocation. Also: worship resources, section for leaders and an excellent list of study resources on a variety of topics.

34. *Respond: Volume 5,* edited by Robert Howard (Judson Press, 1977), 128 pages, $5.95.

Another excellent volume with more helps for youth leaders and many more program subjects, including: Old Testament Prophets, Hunger; series of sessions on Personal Development, Passover. More resources for worship.

35. *Discussion Starters for Youth Groups,* Series 3, by Ann Billups (Judson Press, 1976), 224 pages, $5.95.

Includes many copies of skits which involve common situations, questions, and problems that youth have, plus questions to guide discussion. Also includes suggestions for worship for each skit.

36. *Values Clarification: A Handbook of Practical Strategies for Teachers and Students,* by Sidney B. Simon, Leland W. Howe, and Howard Kirschenbaum (New York: Hart Pub. Co., 1972), 142 pages, $6.95.

79 exercises to help people discover what they believe and value, what's important to them. Very popular with junior and senior highs; excellent discussion starters. Can be used in a study on values or as a means for helping the leaders find out more about their youth.

37. *Making Sense of Our Lives,* by Merrill Harmin (Niles, IL: Argus Communications, 1973), $7.50 per unit.

Values clarification kit appropriate for both junior and senior highs. Could be used effectively in church school, youth group, for retreats or special events. Each of the six units provides materials for six class sessions. Contents: six 14″x21″ color posters, six spirit masters of exercises, six teacher's guides.

38. *Handbook of Serendipity,* by Lyman Coleman (Colorado Springs: Serendipity House, 1976), 96 pages, $4.95.

A collection of 101 of Lyman Coleman's crowd breakers, communication exercises, and Bible studies.

39. *Encyclopedia of Serendipity,* by Lyman Coleman (Serendipity House, 1976), 238 pages, $14.95.

A large collection of the best in the Serendipity series. Includes crowd breakers, communication exercises, Bible study, group building, values clarification, Scripture happenings, Scripture heavies, special group activities.

40. *Youth Elect Series* (YES) of Christian Education: Shared Approaches (Living the Word). 32 pages, $1.75 each.

These are four-to-six-session mini-courses suitable for youth fellowship groups, retreats, lock-ins, summer sessions, and travel conferences. Plans are to have new books published each year.

1978 titles:

Growing Up to Love: Meaning of Sexuality (younger youth)
A Matter of Life and Death (older youth)
Students' Rights (older youth)

1979 titles:

Encountering Prayer and Meditation (younger youth)
Take a Look at Yourself: Book of James (younger youth)
Exploring Other World Religions (older youth)

1980-81 titles:
Who's in Charge? (Of Power and Powerlessness)
(younger youth)

41. *Using Biblical Simulations,* by Donald E. Miller, Graydon F. Snyder, and Robert W. Neff (Judson Press, 1973), 224 pages, $5.95.

Bible study through creative drama simulation. Group is divided in teams which study and prepare to present their point of view on particular crisis situations in the Bible, such as: What shall we do with Jesus?; the Council of Jerusalem; Job and his friends; the Upper Room. Includes five chapters explaining the simulation method and ten actual simulations.

42. *Using Biblical Simulations, Volume 2,* by Donald E. Miller, et al. (Judson Press, 1975), 222 pages, $5.95.

More guidelines for use of simulations. Same format. Topics include: Joseph and His Brothers; Sin at the Door; The Council of Mizpah; The Silversmiths of Ephesus; The House; and more.

43. *Simulation Games for Religious Education,* by Richard Reichert (John Knox Press, 1977), 106 pages, $4.50.

18 actual simulation games using simple resources. Games relate to basic theology, community, the nature of prayer, and moral problems.

44. *Twenty New Ways of Teaching the Bible,* by Donald Griggs (Abingdon, 1977), 80 pages, $4.95.

More creative Bible teaching which includes four simulated Bible activities. Good bibliography.

45. *Alternative Celebrations Catalogue,* 4th edition, edited by Bob Kochtitzky (Alternatives, 1978, P.O. Box 1707, Forest Park, GA 30050), 242 pages, $5.00.

Ideas for creative celebrations of traditional holidays. Includes ideas for making gifts and crafts. Includes an introduction to simple living.

46. *Recycle Catalogue II: Fabulous Flea Market,* by Dennis Benson (Abingdon Press, 1977), 160 pages, $6.95.

A collection of creative ideas for all ages. Divided into four sections: Education and Learning, Fellowship and Community, World and Mission, and Worship and Celebration.

WORSHIP

The following can be used as resources in developing worship services or as devotional resources. When youth are to create their own worship experiences, they can browse through these for ideas for the various parts of the service.

47. *Come, Let Us Celebrate: A Resource Book of Contemporary Worship Services,* by Blair Richards and Janice Sigmund (New York: Hawthorn Books, 1976), 167 pages, $5.95.
26 complete worship services on a variety of themes, in-cluding Advent, Christmas, New Year, Lent, Communion, new members. Also aids to formulating your own celebrations.

48. *New Ways in Worship for Youth: Resources for Twenty Complete Worship Services,* by John Brown (Judson Press, 1969), 224 pages, $5.95.

20 worship services on such themes as: New Year, Lent, Palm Sunday, Easter, Thanksgiving, Advent, Christmas, summer outing, mothers, fathers, youth emphasis, and more.

49. *Ventures in Worship,* edited by David James Randolph (Abingdon), *Volume 1* (1969), $4.95; *Volume 2* (1970), $3.95; *Volume 3* (1973), $3.95.

Excellent resources for worship. Includes calls to worship, prayers, litanies, affirmations of faith, dedications of offerings, ideas for proclamation of the Word, benedictions, special occasions.

50. *Pray, Praise and Hooray,* by Richard Bimler (Concordia, 1972), 114 pages, $3.25.

A collection of "prayers for youth and other people." Prayers developed around "Big Words," such as acceptance, advertisements, baptism, change, confirmation, death, doubt, failure, hunger, hypocrisy, identity, laughter, loneliness, occupation, politics, priorities, war and peace, and others. Well written in the language of youth.

51. *Experiments in Prayer,* by Betsy Caprio (Notre Dame: Ave Maria Press, 1973), 185 pages, $2.95.

Exercises which could be used in youth groups to introduce youth to a variety of prayer experiences—spontaneous prayers, readings, shared prayer, meditations, prayers with music.

52. *Discovery in Prayer,* by Robert J. Heyer and Richard J. Payne (Paulist Press, 1969), 144 pages, $2.50.

A part of the Discovery series, includes prayers and quotes on communication, freedom, love, peace, life, and happiness.

53. *Tune In,* edited by Herman C. Ahrens, Jr. (Philadelphia: Pilgrim Press, 1968), 96 pages, $2.95.

Collection of prayers reflecting concerns of young people. Could be used in worship, discussion, or dramatic presentation.

54. *He Is the Still Point of the Turning World,* by Mark Link (Argus Communications, 1971), 120 pages, $4.95.

A compilation of poems, scriptures, and quotes depicting Jesus Christ as our still-, reference-, focal-, touch-, pivotal-, and decision-point in the various aspects of our lives.

55. *In the Stillness Is the Dancing,* by Mark Link (Argus Communications, 1972), 120 pages, $4.95.
A similar compilation as the book above.

56. *Love Is a Magic Penny: Meditations for Junior Highs,* by Tom Neufer Emswiler (Abingdon, 1977), 111 pages, $3.95.
111 excellent devotions. Includes Scripture and meditations on the theme of love.

57. *Creative Brooding,* by Robert Raines (New York: Macmillan, 1977), 116 pages, $1.95 pb.

A collection of readings appropriate for use in worship experiences. Excellent devotional material.

58. *Soundings,* by Robert Raines (Word Books, 1970), 144 pages, $3.95 pb.

Another collection similar to the above.

59. *Psalms/Now,* by Leslie F. Brandt (Concordia, 1973), 222 pages, $5.95.

A paraphrase of the psalms which turns them into prayers for a contemporary world, using words, phrases, and the look of today.

60. *Epistles/Now,* by Leslie E. Brandt (Concordia, 1976), 187 pages, $6.95.

Similar to the above, this book is a paraphrase of Paul's letters.

As a part of Ministry Within the Congregation, the youth can lead children in worship experiences, including a "children's sermon" during Sunday morning services. The following are two resources to aid in leading worship with children:

61. *Liturgies for Little Ones: 38 Complete Celebrations for Kindergarten Through Third Grade,* by Carol Rezy (Ave Maria Press, 1978), 159 pages, $3.95.

All that is needed for planning and leading liturgies for young elementary children is in this creative volume. Includes many ideas for banners and posters.

62. *Little Threads and Other Object Lessons for Children,* by Harvey Daniel Moore (Abingdon Press, 1974), 80 pages, $3.95.

31 sermons for children using simple objects to illustrate the message.

SONGBOOKS

63. *Songs,* by Yohann Anderson (San Anselmo, CA: Songs and Creations, 1978), 185 pages, $3.95.

Great collection of over 500 songs (folk songs, hymns, folk hymns, spirituals, oldie-goldies, some standards). Songbook includes lyrics and guitar chords ($3.95). Complete music is available in loose-leaf notebook ($13.95).

64. *The Avery and Marsh Songbook,* by Richard Avery and Donald Marsh (Port Jervis, NY: Proclamation Productions, Inc., 1972), $2.95 for lyrics and chords; $6.95 for complete music.

Includes all 61 hymns and carols from: *Hymns Hot and Carols Cool; More, More, More; Alive and Singing; Songs for the Search; Songs for the Easter People.* All original songs.

65. *Songbook for Saints and Sinners,* compiled by Carolton R. Young (Carol Stream, IL: Agape, 1973), $1.00 for pocket-size; $4.95 for spiral edition.

66. *The Genesis Songbook,* compiled by Carlton R. Young (Agape, 1973), $1.50 for pocket-size; $5.95 for spiral edition.

67. *The Exodus Songbook,* compiled by Carlton R. Young (Agape, 1973), $1.50 for pocket-size; $6.95 for spiral edition.

The above three are excellent little songbooks for youth groups. They include many familiar folk songs and folk hymns. The newer songs are well written.

68. *Ventures in Songs,* edited by David J. Randolph (Abingdon Press, 1972), 126 pages, $2.95.

A songbook which marks a positive move toward updating the songs of today's church.

69. *Hymnals for Young Christians* (Los Angeles, CA: F.E.L. Publications).

Volume 1 (1966, 1975)—186 folk hymns. $4.50.
Volume 2 (1970)—136 folk hymns. Includes 69 songs from *Volume 1.* $4.00.
Volume 3 (1973)—125 folk hymns. $4.00.

DRAMA

70. *Happy Tales, Fables, and Plays,* by Gordon C. Bennett (John Knox Press, 1975), $5.95.

16 delightful short plays for two, three, or four voices. They are to be done "readers theatre" style. The book provides a copy of each play for each reader. Could be used by youth during worship services or at a congregational function. Discussion questions are provided at the end of each play.

71. *Readers Theatre Comes to Church,* by Gordon C. Bennett (John Knox Press, 1972), 128 pages, $4.95.

A complete guide to the form of drama called "readers theatre." Includes how to find and prepare materials, how to develop capable interpreters, and how to stage. Also includes five sample scripts.

72. *Celebrate with Drama: Dramas and Meditations for Six Special Days,* by W.A. Poovey (Minneapolis: Augsburg, 1975), 128 pages, $2.95.

Six plays for Easter, Ascension Day, Pentecost, Mission Sunday, Fellowship Sunday, and Thanksgiving.

73. *Contemporary Drama Service.* One of the best sources for drama materials, including plays for chancel or fellowship room, productions, plays with slides, musicals, musical dance dramas, choral readings, folk rock liturgies, excellent Christmas and Easter presentations, coffee house materials, and skits. For a catalog, write to:

Contemporary Drama Service
P.O. Box 457
Downers Grove, IL 60515

MAGAZINES

74. *YOUTH Magazine.* Monthly magazine for senior highs which probes the feelings behind the facts and takes the time to listen, to understand. Includes articles relevant to teens of today. Single subscription $8.25 a year; three or more to one address $1.65 each, quarterly, and receive YOUTH PLUS in addition, which is a leader's guide for using the current issue of YOUTH.

Order from: YOUTH Magazine
10 Pelham Parkway
Pelham Manor, NY 10803

75. *Alive!* Similar to YOUTH Magazine, only geared to grades 7-8. Attractive photographs and art work illustrate the magazine. $6.50 for single subscription; three or more to one address $3.00 each for a six-month semester; three or more to one address $1.55 each, per quarter. Single copy 60¢.

Order from: ALIVE Magazine
Christian Board of Publication
Box 179
St. Louis, MO 63166

76. *MASS MEDIA NEWSLETTER,* edited by Clifford J. York. Monthly newsletter giving reviews, editorials, and guides for upcoming media resources (commercial films, television, filmstrips) for educational use in the church. $10 per year ($13 for first class).

Order from: Mass Media Ministries, Inc.
2116 North Charles Street
Baltimore, MD 21218

ADDRESSES FOR RESOURCE CATALOGS

Argus Communications
7440 Natchez Avenue
Niles, IL 60608

Insight Films
Paulist Productions
Box 1057
Pacific Palisades, CA 90272

MARK IV
La Salette
Enfield, NH 03748

Rev. Floyd Shaffer (Clown Ministry)
Faith and Fantasy
32185 Susi Lane
Roseville, MI 48066

NTEP (National Teacher Education Project)
6947 East Granada Road
Scottsdale, AZ 85253

TeleKETICS *and* TeleSLIDES
Franciscan Communications Center
1229 South Santee Street
Los Angeles, CA 90015

KAIROS (KAIROS News)
Box 24056
Minneapolis, MN 55424

Appendix A

The Difference Between This Book and
The Exuberant Years

Those of you who are familiar with *The Exuberant Years: A Guide for Junior High Leaders* (John Knox Press, 1976), which I wrote several years ago, will recognize the planning process (chapter 4, *The Exuberant Years,* pp. 21-42). In it I used the same approach described here, that is, the five-category, balanced program for youth ministry.

The Exuberant Years model had two extra steps which made it a much more complicated process. The first was the writing of a *diagnosis,* which was written by the youth leaders, based on their observation of their group of youth. They were to note what the youth were like, their needs, what kind of relationships the youth had with each other, with adults, with parents.

This diagnosis was then to be shared with the group, prefaced by "This is the way I (adult leader) see this group." I cautioned against making the diagnosis personal. Example: "There is one youth who has problems at home." Rather, it was to be about the group in general. I encouraged humor, which is helpful if there are negative comments involved.

I have omitted the diagnosing from this book's approach for several reasons. No matter how careful they tried to be, leaders were reporting that this was too threatening. Many items can be taken personally.

There are negative aspects in a diagnosis. I now think that we need to eliminate as much of the negative as possible from our relationship with youth.

It was also asking new leaders, people who did not really know these youth, to make a diagnosis, to put a value judgment on their observation of the youth group. New leaders should not be placed in this position. It could affect their relationship to the group.

Diagnosing, if defined as discovering what our needs are as a group, can and should be done after the first year. It is suggested in chapter 14 of this book that youth and adult leaders work at this during an evaluation of the year.

The second extra step is *goal setting.* Did I actually omit goal setting from this leadership team approach? Yes and no. Determining directions and goals is an essential part of any program within the church. In this new approach the goal is general: that all youth be involved in the total life of the church.

Broken down into the five categories, it proposes five separate goals:

That all youth—

1. be involved in the worship of the church
2. be involved in the study aspects of the church's life
3. have opportunities to share in ministering to and with the congregation
4. be involved in service to the community
5. have opportunities for fellowship with others of their own age group

These are workable, useful goals not only for youth ministry, but for Christian education in general, for all ages in the life of the church.

This approach provides this general, valid goal to give basic direction to youth ministry. The problem in *The Exuberant Years* was that the youth and leaders were to brainstorm a variety of goals and then brainstorm a variety of alternatives under each of the goals.

This extra step of brainstorming goals caused

much confusion. It was reported that the planning broke down in the process of formulating goals and trying to choose from among these goals. It is difficult for young people to think in terms of goals and to articulate the objectives they want for their group.

After this leadership team approach has been in action for a couple of years, the youth will have had opportunities to be involved in decision-making, as responsible persons and in other leadership roles. Then, evaluation of needs and projection of possible goals can take place. But if your youth program is struggling and looking for new life, goal setting as described in *The Exuberant Years* may only make the planning process more complicated.

Another difference is that in *The Exuberant Years,* it was suggested that the planning be done in a three-hour meeting. From the responses of people who were using the planning process, it became evident that effective planning could not be done in a three-hour meeting. The placing of items on the calendar is done at such a hectic pace that when the meeting is over, no one knows what was planned. It happens too fast.

Also, there is little time for group building, which is necessary to create a relaxed, congenial atmosphere in which to do effective planning. The retreat setting emerged as a must. It offers the kind of time needed for group building and a better pace for planning. With the leadership team approach, the retreat is essential, for the leaders need the time to get to know the youth. It is easier to work together when you know each other.

One other difference: *The Exuberant Years* was written primarily for junior highs, although the planning process is designed to be used with both junior and senior highs. This book is written for both groups and recommends that each group have its own coordinator, leaders, and calendar of activities.

Appendix B

Idea Lists Under Each of the Five Categories

The most frequent request I get is for ideas—program ideas. At most of my workshops I encourage youth leaders to share ideas that have worked in their churches. They fill out the five-category form used in chapter 5 to evaluate their own youth ministry. I have been collecting these ideas for the past four years.

In the next few pages are the lists of activities in each of the five categories. There is no explanation for the items. They are presented here merely to give you *ideas.* Let your imagination and creativity loose. You should be able to come up with all kinds of activities.

Consider making a shorter list of ideas under each category for recruiters to take on their recruiting visits.

WORSHIP

During Sunday morning service
 — Call to worship, scripture
 — Prayers, offering
 — Mini-drama
 — Use of audio-visuals
 — Puppets
 — Music, musical
 — Instrumental music
 — Role play
 — Dance
 — Act out parable
 — Usher, acolyte

Regular attendance
Youth do entire service
Palm procession
Passover
Jewish Seder
Children's sermons

Design and lead worship service for children
Design and lead worship for vacation church school
Make banners
Outdoor worship
Easter sunrise service
Youth choir
Conduct prayer service
Christmas program
Advent wreath lighting during worship service
Advent church school services
 (15 minute service at beginning of church school for 4
 Sundays in Advent)
Make chrismons for chrismon tree
Lenten services
Worship after football game
Worship at retreats or lock-ins
Lead worship for elderly
Design and lead early Sunday morning family service
Visit other churches
Handbell choir
Write on 3 x 5 cards thoughts or prayers for use in worship
Worship in catacombs (simulating early Christians)
Write hymns and songs (write words to familiar hymn or
 song tune)
Agape Meal/Agape Feast (a worship experience designed
 around a meal, after the Moravian tradition)
Worship workshop
Live nativity scene
New Year's Eve service
Clown ministry, Floyd Shaffer–style (see address in
 chapter 17)
Prayer at congregational functions
Hymn of the month (youth research and publish information
 in bulletin or newsletter)
Design and conduct worship at church picnic

STUDY

Church school curriculum topics
Other denominations
Worship
Social issues
Death
Death and dying (grief process)
Parent/youth relations
Other religions
Christian lifestyle at school
Lifestyle
    — Simplicity
    — Conservation
School
Hunger
Poverty
Environmental concerns
Christian living
Friendship
Prayer and meditation
Living the faith
The Ten Commandments
Beatitudes
Twenty-third Psalm
Apostles' Creed
Passover and Holy Week

Baptism and the Lord's Supper
Moses
Men of the Covenant—Old Testament
Value process
Values clarification
Identity
Relationships
Jobs as Christian vocations
Career exploration
Making decisions
Handling conflict
Mark
Life and teachings of Jesus
Meaning of Jesus Christ
Bible quiz
People who encountered Jesus
Prepare mini-course for children
Bible study at coffee house
Bible study at retreat
Mini-course at retreat
Music
    — Modern
    — Church
    — Hymns
    — Christmas carols
Discussion of sermons
Science fiction

Study related to lectionary
Counseling center testing
Lenten studies
— Ash Wednesday
— Passion
— Good Friday
— Palm Sunday
— Easter
Eternal life and other options
The arts
Evangelism
Global concerns
Why poverty?
Spirituality
Confirmation/commissioning
Women of the Bible
Seasons of the church year
Shorter Catechism
Field trips
Prophets
Prophecy
Paul
Puppetry workshop
Bible workshop
Communication workshop
Intergenerational studies
— On honesty
— Communication
— Values
— Biblical
Atlernate celebrations
Love
Romans
Galatians
Who is God?
What is a Christian?
Presbyterian heritage
Presbyterian beliefs

Sex/sexuality
Dating
Marriage
Overview of the Bible
Alcohol
Drugs
Capital punishment
Criminal justice
Revelation
Weekly Bible study (outside of church school)
Caravan trip
Symbols
Movies
Visual arts
Youth problems
Commitment
Biblical simulations
Building a Christian community
Success
Our church's life
Community concerns
Prejudice/racism
Forgiveness
Students' rights
The occult
Parables
Stewardship
Violence
Censorship (TV, magazines, etc.)
Women's movement

MINISTRY WITHIN THE CONGREGATION

Help with vacation Bible school
— Teaching
— Recreation

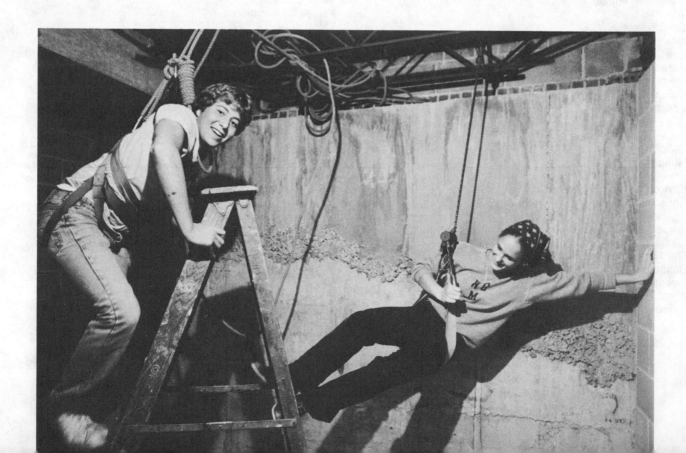

— Music
— Refreshments
— Nursery for VBS teachers
Help prepare church school materials
Make visual aids for teachers
Team teaching in church school
Serving in the nursery and extended session
Easter sunrise breakfast
Pancake breakfast
Buffet luncheon
Serve at church dinners
Restaurant for congregational dinner
Design mini-course for children
Lead Advent workshop for children
Church school substitute
Work with elderly and shut-ins

— Bake cookies and make containers out of oatmeal boxes
— Birthday cards, make gifts
— Make emergency telephone numbers book
— Adopt a grandma/pa
— Clean yards and odd jobs
— Run errands
— Take them shopping
— Telephone check-in

Tape ministry for shut-ins and hospitalized
Youth choir
Cantata with adult choir
Musicals
Dramas
Acolytes, ushers
Mothers' Morning Out during Christmas vacation
Craft fair
Fun Night for family night dinner (youth lead all activities: recreation, group-building games, values exercises)
Run A-V equipment
Catalog visual aids for church school
Youth visit youth (a welcome wagon for new youth)
New member assimilation (assign-a-youth)
Play piano or organ for accompaniment
Work with children's choir
Recreation and parties for children
Big brother/big sister for children (youth are big brother/sister to individual elementary children of the church)
Halloween party for children (spook house)
Serve on committees/task forces
— Evaluation committees
— Pulpit committees
Forum on leadership roles in the church
Intergenerational studies
Parent night/parent reception
Adult/youth seminars on topics
Adult/youth bowling teams, volleyball, softball
Serve ice cream at church dinner
Ice cream social (Mother's Day)
Carnivals
Mission fair (with meal of that country)
Caroling (either to members' homes or with adults)
Design and prepare bulletin boards
Car wash
Yard work for members
Talent show

Bake and serve cookies between church school and church (with all youth present—emphasis on visibility)
Tutoring
Help with worship
Clean church yard
Slave Day, Rent-a-Senior
Live nativity
Easter egg hunt for children
Decorate church (Christmas)
Banners
Puppet show
— Have puppet workshop for youth. They then present show for children or for congregational dinner.
Sponsor special food collection (collect from congregation for local needy families)
Present special programs or displays on study topics
Video presentation on church or church school, or on seasons of the church year
Interview adult classes (with or without tape recorder)
Do recreation at church picnic
Make posters for various emphases
— Christian education
— Youth ministry

SERVICE

Neighborhood cleanup
City cleanup
Take care of lawns for elderly
— Rake leaves
Adopt a child (locally or overseas)
— Big Brother/Big Sister
Sponsor needy families
Toys for poor at Christmas
Give program for senior citizens
— Christmas
— Puppets
— Anytime
Craft projects to make gifts for elderly
Clown ministry
Brainstorm ongoing service to elderly
— Birthday cards
— Writing letters for them
— Singing
— Checking on (telephoning)
— Doing errands
— Taking them shopping
Help with Meals on Wheels
Fast for CROP
CROP walk (CROP is the hunger program of Church World Service, Box 968, Elkhart, Indiana 46514.)
Parties or picnic for children's homes or retarded children's center
Singing for convalescent homes
Summer program for preschoolers in low-income neighborhood
Day camp in low-income neighborhood
Helping with Girls' or Boys' Club
Tutoring
UNICEF collection
Puppet shows for children

Help in library
     — Saturday reading program
Shovel snow
Work camps
Urban camps
Teen center
Coffee house
Agency aides (Red Cross, Girls' Club)
Visits in day care centers
Summer aiding in day care
Food and clothing collection and distribution
Recycling paper and aluminum cans
Education of community on social concerns by displays or
     presentation (connected to a study youth have done)
Help with city recreation program
Christmas for prisoners
     — Make stockings and fill with toothbrushes, etc.
Invite non–church-related friends to activities

FELLOWSHIP

Retreats
Lock-ins (church-ins)
Movies
Eat (burger or pizza place)
Trips
Car caravans
Beach
Snow skiing
Water skiing
Talent show

Camping
Cold (rough) camping
Skating
Bicycling
Bowling
Caroling
Craft workshops
Craft projects
Refreshments in homes
Progressive dinners
Parties
     — Halloween
     — Valentine
Coffee house
Sports
     — With other groups
     — Baseball, softball
     — Volleyball, soccer
     — Basketball
Recreation (games)
Retreats with other church youth groups
Youth singing groups
Singing
Hayrides
Horseback riding
Swimming
Cookouts
Hikes
Square dance
Museums
Scavenger hunt
Polaroid scavenger hunt
Denominational youth conferences (synod, presbytery,
     district)
District camps
Youth rallies
Work camps
Community cultural events
Dances
Dance after football or basketball game
Jogging
TV viewing
Rafting
Canoe trips
Mimes
Carnival
Mission fair
Crab soccer
Miniature golf
Ping pong
Pool
Trip to a college for a day
Rock concerts
Sailing
Values mini-course
Group-building activities
Cook dinner for parents
This Is Your Life

Appendix C

Group-Building Activities

Group builders are activities which facilitate interaction in a group. It is hard for youth to walk up to kids they do not know and carry on a conversation. Group builders are games or exercises which, through a structure, help people relate to each other. You could say they gently force people to get to know each other.

Many of these exercises are "ice breakers" and are used at the very beginning of a meeting to help people feel comfortable being in the group. Kids who are shy or feel like outsiders need something to get them involved with the group. Group builders "break the ice."

Group builders are also used to "build a group." A common concern of leaders is that their youth group is not becoming a group. It is essential in youth ministry to use methods which gradually teach young people to care for each other. In order to develop a more caring group, we use get-acquainted exercises, followed by more in-depth methods. Games and recreation also aid in the development of a caring group.

The following are activities which can be used throughout the year. Some, such as the first eight, are specifically used as introductions, ways to learn each other's names. The creative names tags give kids a chance to tell each other a little bit about themselves.

These activities can be used at regular meetings, at retreats, in church school, wherever. They are not solely for the beginning of the year. Some, such as open-ended statements, can be used throughout the year in relation to studies or issues. Others are beneficial when new youth join the group.

The task of building a group never stops. Group builders should be included at most occasions throughout the year.

Leaders and Coordinators: Become familiar with these activities. I have listed the ones that I have actually used. There are many more to be found in programmatic materials.

Lyman Coleman, who is a master at group building, has created hundreds of techniques for building and maintaining groups. He is the author of the Serendipity series (*Acts Alive, Groups in Action, Celebration, Discovery, Breaking Free, 10-4 Good Buddy, Breaker 1-9, Movin' On,* and others). Most of the books in this series are mini-courses in various aspects of self-discovery and Christian living. He has two books which are compilations of group-building activities: *Encyclopedia of Serendipity* (no. 39 in chapter 17), and *Handbook of Serendipity* (no. 38). Some of the following are taken from these two books.

Introduction Activities

1. Introduction Interview

Pass out paper and pencils to everyone. Have each person get together with someone he or she does not know (or know very well). Everyone should have a partner.

Instructions: You are to interview your partner to find out as much as you can about him or her in six minutes—where he/she was born, favorite food, hobby, TV show, likes, dislikes—whatever you would like to ask. Jot all this down on paper.

Obviously, you are to be interviewing each other at the same time. Keep firing questions at each other and writing down information.

After six or seven minutes, call time. Have everyone gather in one group if you have fourteen or less people. If you have more, split into groups of eight to ten each. Ask someone to start by introducing to the group the person he/she interviewed. Go around the circle until everyone has been introduced.

2. Simple Introductions

Instead of the familiar "State your name, age, and school," have everyone introduce himself/herself by stating:

name, school, favorite food, favorite TV show

You could also use:

favorite singing group, favorite restaurant, favorite animal

Think of more!

3. Descriptive Name Tags

Have all members of the group take a piece of construction paper (at least 6" x 10") and a felt pen. They are to write their names across the top in large letters. Then, have them write four or five words describing themselves (their interests, attributes). However, the words must end in "-ing" or "-able." For example: "tennisable," "sillying," "fluteable." The words need not be real words, but they must have "-ing" or "-able" tacked on the end. They should write these words anywhere on the paper on the same side as their names. Have them pin on their name tags or wear them with string hanging around their necks.

Now, they are to roam around the room, reading everyone's name tag, asking questions about the words.

4. Name Tag Symbols[1]

Have all members of the group take a piece of paper. They are to think of four interests they have, four things that are very important to them at the present. Draw a symbol for each of the four on the name tag paper. They should also put their names somewhere on the paper. Have them pin on the name tags. When everyone has finished, have each person describe his or her name tag to the group. If your group is larger than fourteen, split into two or more groups.

5. Name Tag Collage[2]

As individuals arrive, explain that they are to make a name tag collage. They are each to cut a piece of construction paper in any shape they wish. Then, direct them to piles of magazines, newspapers, and glue. They are to find five or six pictures or words that would tell something about "who they are." After they have finished, they should put string through the name tags and wear them around their necks.

When everyone is finished, they are to introduce themselves to the group by describing the collages.

6. Name Anagrams

Using colored construction paper for name tags, have everyone write his or her first name down the left side of the paper. They are to think of characteristics about themselves or interests they have that start with the letters of their names. They are to write these words next to the appropriate letters.

7. Zip Zap

Zip Zap is a circle game designed for learning first names. The participants must know who is seated to their left and to their right. The person on your left is your ZIP. The person on your right is your ZAP. The leader stands in the center of the circle. He or she points to a person and says: "ZIP, one, two, three, four, five." That person must shout out the name of the person to his/her left (or ZIP) within the count of five. If the leader points to a person and says: "ZAP, one, two, three, four, five," that person must shout the name of the person to his/her right (or ZAP). If the person pointed to fails, he or she takes the leader's place in the center of the circle. The leader takes that person's chair.

8. John, John, John

This is an exercise for review of names. The leader stands in the middle of the circle. Everyone is seated on the floor or in chairs. The leader flips around the circle, pointing at different people. When the leader points, everyone says that person's name in a resounding chorus four times. When a name comes a little slowly to the group, the leader should stand over that person and point, point, point, until everyone is saying, "Fred, Fred, Fred, Fred," with assurance. For fun, keep going back to one person.

Large Group Fun Times

9. Can't Say No!

Everyone is given ten beans. The object is to take beans from persons by getting them to say "no," "nothing," "uh-uh," "never." Tell everyone to mill around the room asking questions of each other. They can be questions about anything, hopefully about something for which they will receive a negative response.

Each time an individual gets someone to say "no" or something negative, he or she takes one of that person's beans. Allow the game to go on for ten minutes. The person with the most beans wins.

10. Who Am I?

Preparation: Make a set of stick-on name tags with the name of a famous person on each. Make enough for everybody.

Stick a name tag on each person's back and instruct participants not to tell people who they are. All are to mingle and ask questions about who they are.

Rules: Questions must be answered by "yes" or "no." And you cannot ask the same person another question. You must move around, asking different people questions.

When you discover who are you, call it out. See how long it takes for the first person to discover who he or she is. Play this game until all participants guess who they are.

Suggestions for names:

Donald Duck	The Lone Ranger
Thomas Jefferson	Kermit the Frog
Albert Einstein	Lassie
Noah	The Incredible Hulk
Pooh Bear	John F. Kennedy
Burt Reynolds	Julius Caesar
Jane Fonda	Tarzan
Dolly Parton	Rip Van Winkle
Jimmy Conners	Three Little Pigs
O.J. Simpson	Henry VIII
Muhammed Ali	Al Capone
Romeo	Superman
Juliet	Shakespeare
Archie Bunker	Jack the Ripper
Little Red Riding Hood	Napoleon
Pope John Paul II	Harry S. Truman
Queen Elizabeth	Snoopy
Peter Pan	Charlie Brown
Scrooge	Big Bird

Think of more!

11. Sign My Card

Mimeograph a list of items, such as the following:

A girl with six stuffed animals at home
Uses Ban roll-on
Sings in the shower
Has a relative living in New York
Jogs at least three times a week
Reads the newspaper every day
Weighs between 120 and 125
Wears socks to bed
Has never babysat
Has had tonsils taken out
Can play bridge
Reads *The National Enquirer*
Went to church school last Sunday
Loves spinach
Saw Cecil B. DeMille's *The Ten Commandments*
Is taller than his/her mother
Has two sisters
Eats Cheerios for breakfast
Has won a trophy
Likes graham crackers
Is taking French in school
Likes Breakfast Squares

Give each person a sheet. They are to mingle around in the room, finding people who fit the statements. When they do, for example, find a "girl who has six stuffed animals at home," they have her sign her name next to the appropriate statement.

They are to try to get as many different names as possible. See who fills the card first.

12. Mingle

Have everybody mingle in the room, that is, walk around fairly close to one another. The leader calls out a number, say "four." Everybody forms groups of four and freezes. The leader walks around eliminating any groups which have more or less than four. The game continues until there are only two people left.

Variation: No elimination. Just form groups according to the number called by the leader. When group is formed, each person tells his/her name to the group.

Games for Groups of 8 to 15

13. Name Charade[3]

Prepare a stack of stick-on name tags with names of characters, movie stars, celebrities, politicians, etc.

Stick one name on the back of one person in the group. Everyone looks at this name and pantomimes the character, until the person guesses the name. No talking or sounds of any kind—strictly pantomime.

For names, see the list of names under *Who Am I?*, #10.

14. Machines[4]

Each group is to make a machine which has movable parts. Every part (person) must move in some way. The machine can be authentic, such as an airplane, a cuckoo clock, or a pinball machine. Or it could be "just a machine"—with gears, levers, pumps, etc.

Let each group demonstrate its machine.

15. A What?[5]

There are several versions of this game. One is to start an object around the circle to the left saying, "This is a dog." Next person says, "A what?" Starter

says, "A dog." The object is then passed to the next person with the same procedure, but "A what?" question is always relayed back to the starter, who in turn gives the answer, which is relayed back around the circle, gradually repeated a number of times.

Simultaneous with starting "dog" to the left, the leader starts "cat" to the right, with same procedure.

A popular version is to have a several-word description, like "A freshly baked peach pie" and "A jar of watermelon pickles," or "This is a shawl with a long fringe" and "This is a pair of galoshes, slightly worn but wearable." (The longer the line, the smaller the circle should be to enjoy it.)

The fun comes when signals for "dog" and "cat" begin to cross each other halfway around circle, and players do not know which way to turn for "A what?"

Any object can be used, such as a salt shaker for the dog and a pepper shaker for the cat.

This is a great game to use when having youth and adults together.

16. One Frog[6]

This is a game of math (simple math). Divide into groups of equal numbers. The object is to get to ten frogs, using the following system: The first person in the circle says, "one frog"; the next person says, "two eyes"; the next, "four legs"; the next, "in the pond"; the next, "kerplunk"; and the next, "kerplunk."

Then, the next person says, "two frogs"; the next person, "four eyes"; the next, "eight legs"; the next,

"in the pond"; the next, "in the pond"; the next, "kerplunk"; the next, "kerplunk"; the next, "kerplunk"; and the next, "kerplunk."

There is one "in the pond" and two "kerplunks" for every frog.

If you make a mistake, the next person starts over with, "one frog." The group to reach ten frogs wins.

17. Grand Prix Races

This is a circle game, similar to "One Frog." Divide into small groups of equal numbers. This is a series of four races to see who can make it around the track first.

The first race is Jalopies. Jalopies go "putt putt." So the first person says "putt putt," the next says "putt putt," the next, "putt putt" all around the circle eight times. The first person should keep track of the laps as they are completed.

You will need to go as fast as you can without skipping anyone. The first group to complete the eight laps lets out a whoop.

The second race is XKE's. And they go "vrooooom." So each person says "vroooom," again imitating a car going around a track. Again, eight laps.

The last race is Motorboats. Motorboats go: "plplplhh." I can't spell it, but it is done by putting your tongue between your lips and blowing. You may need to shield your mouth with your hands to keep from spraying each other. This sound is to go around the track eight laps.

The Grand Prix is the fourth and last race. It consists of 24 laps—8 of Jalopies (putt putt), 8 of XKE's (vroooom), and 8 of Motorboats (plplplhh).

Small Group Exercises

Numbers 18 through 24 are best used in small groups of four or five youth.

18. In Event of Fire[7]

This exercise concerns what one values in life. Tell the group to imagine that each of their houses is on fire and they have only three minutes to save their most valuable possessions.

What four things (other than people) would you try to save? Go around the circle, letting each person list his or her four items. Ask them to explain why they chose those particular items.

19. Guess Who?[8]

This group builder is a game that gives more information about individuals. It is best played in a group that has been together for a while.

Pass out slips of paper and pencils, and 3" x 5" cards. Have each person put his or her answers to the following questions on the slip of paper:

1. Where were you born?
2. Where is the farthest place you have ever visited?
3. What is your favorite song?
4. What did you want to be when you were a child?

After everyone has finished, collect the slips. You are going to read a slip, Number 1. They are to guess who they think wrote the answers on that slip of paper and write that name on their card for Number 1. Then read the second slip, and so forth.

After you have read them all, go back to Number 1, read it again, and ask who they put down. After the shouting of names, ask the person who did write it to confess. How many were right?

20. Four Facts/One Lie[9]

Each person in the small group is to write answers to four questions. Three of the answers are to be true and one is to be a lie. Read the following four questions:

1. What is the farthest place you've been from home?
2. What is a dumb thing you did?
3. What is something you were not supposed to do as a child, but did anyway?
4. What is your favorite song?

They can lie about any one they want to. Have them write down their answers.

Have someone begin by reading his or her four answers. Let the others in the group guess which one is the lie. After all have guessed, the person tells which was the lie.

21. Stranded on an Island

Suppose you were stranded on an island and could have your wish for four things, anything you wanted. Have persons in the group list the four things they would wish for. Then let them read their answers.

22. A Special Dinner

If you could have a special dinner to which you could invite five famous people, who would you invite? Everyone should make a list and then share it with the group.

23. Open-ended Statements

These are single-answer statements which can be used for a variety of group-building, value-oriented, or study-related activities.

Make the statement and go around the circle, letting each person complete the statement.

The following are suggestions for open-ended statements. Make up some of your own.

My favorite thing to do on a Saturday . . .
The thing I don't like about Sundays . . .
The room I like best in my house is . . .
If I could work for six months anywhere in the world . . .
A place I would like to visit . . .
If I had $500,000 given to me, I would . . .
I am proud of . . .
What makes me angry . . .
I am happiest when . . .
People can hurt my feelings by . . .
I can't stand . . .
A crazy thing I did as a child . . .
Something I did when my parents told me not to . . .
At age 10 or 11 my hero was . . .
If I were in a circus I would be . . .
If I were in a zoo, I would be . . .
The thing I like best about school is . . .
The thing I like least about school is . . .
To improve my school, I would . . .
The most important quality in a friendship is . . .
An adult (besides parents) who means a lot to me is . . .
I am good at . . .

Something I worry about is . . .
I wish my parents would . . .
Being a Christian means . . .
The hardest decisions I have to make have to do with . . .
If I have children, I want them to . . .
If I could have lunch with anyone, it would be . . .
Something I am afraid of is . . .
My favorite thing to do on a vacation is . . .
A quality I would like to have is . . .
If I had a CB handle, it would be . . .
If I had a T-shirt designed, it would say . . .

24. Think of . . .

Similar to open-ended statements, use the following:

Think of an animal that would describe who you are.
Think of three silly fears you had as a child.
Think of three crazy dreams you had as a child of what you wanted to be or do when you grew up.
Think of three big disappointments you had as a child.

Think of more!

25. Virginia Reel Conversation

This is a fun way to encourage listening on a one-to-one basis. Have everyone line up Virginia Reel style—two lines of equal length. Sit on the floor (or in chairs) with lines facing each other, a foot apart.

You have a list of questions or open-ended statements (see no. 23 for suggestions). Ask the first question. The pairs have two or three minutes to talk with each other about that question, each giving the other his or her answer.

Call time. Only one line moves. That line moves to the left one person. The end person comes down and fills the empty space at the other end. Each person has a new conversation partner. The leader reads the next question. Again, each person talks with the person opposite for two or three minutes. Time is called. The line moves to the left again, and so on.

Ideas for Getting into Groups

Instead of counting off and having all the "ones" be a group, and the "twos," and so forth, or having colored name tags be the guide for grouping, you could do a couple of creative activities:

26. Animals

Pass out pieces of paper that have the names of animals on them—pig, horse, cow, dog, cat, duck, turkey, rooster—animals that make sounds.

At a signal, each person makes the sound of his/her animal. All cows become a group, all cats a group, etc.

27. Songs

Prepare slips of paper with song titles. Have eight of each title (if you plan to have groups of eight). At a signal, all sing their songs as loud as they can. They look for others singing the same song and form small groups.

Use nursery rhymes, little kid songs, and Christmas songs—something simple.

28. Who Am I?

Play "Who Am I?" (no. 10); except prepare eight stick-on name tags of each name (for groups of eight). Instruct them, once they find out who they are, to look for others with the same name. Thus, small groups are formed.

Value-Related Exercises

Value-related exercises make good group builders. All of the following can be used with the total group.

29. Stand on Numbers

This is a "strength of feeling" exercise, which is very popular with kids. They have nicknamed it "Stand on Numbers."

Pass out paper and pencils. Have the youth copy a list of words, such as:

Football	Church
Politics	Police
School	Soap operas
Women's Lib	(name of TV show)
Censorship	(popular singer)

Substitute words relating to current issues.

For each word, they are to choose the number that identifies their feelings about the word and write it down after the word. A "1" indicates strongly *negative* feelings. A "7" indicates strongly *positive* feelings. Caution them to try to stay away from "4," which is the middle-of-the-road number. If, however, there is a word for which they have no feeling one way or the other, then they would write a "4."

While the participants are working on this, the leader takes numbered sheets (or cards) and places them

on the floor, about two or three feet apart, in a straight line.

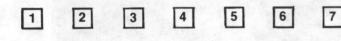

After everyone has finished writing, show them where the numbers are. Explain that they are going to have an opportunity to "take a stand" on issues and see how they compare with others in the group. Have them take their sheets with them.

While they are moving toward the numbers, call out the first word. They should move to the appropriate number. They need stand there only a few seconds, long enough to look around the room and see the distribution of the group.

Call the next word . . . and so on.

30. More Hamburger than Steak

In this exercise participants are to determine which extreme is more like the way they see themselves.

"Are you more hamburger than steak?" The leader asks all those who are more "hamburger" to go to this side of the room. All those who are more "steak" are to go to the opposite side of the room.

Once they have reached their sides, everyone is to pair up with someone else there and discuss why they are more "hamburger" or "steak."

Use the following and make up some of your own:

hamburger	steak
country	city
television	books
leader	follower
pioneer	settler
giver	receiver
breakfast	supper
spectator	participant
early-riser	late-nighter
mountains	beach
tiger	kitty cat
clown	straight man
country western	classical
Cadillac	Volkswagen
spender	saver

31. How Many of You. . . ?

This is a fun exercise in which youth express their likes, dislikes, and how they feel about certain issues.

The leader reads a question. Participants raise their hands according to the strength of their feelings. If the answer is "yes" or "strongly in favor," they raise their hands high. If they are "against," they hold their arms down by their sides. If "in the middle," they hold their arms straight out in front at a 90 degree angle to their bodies.

After the voting, proceed to the next question.

Questions:

How many of you . . .

have ever been in an airplane?
would like to go up in an airplane?

would like to go up in a single-engine, small plane?
like Breakfast Squares?
like to cook?
have to cook?
know what career you would like to pursue?
would hitchhike?
would pick up a hitchhiker?
have ever stolen anything?
have ever signed a petition?
have ever written a letter to your congressperson?
would like to write a letter to your congressperson?
watch soap operas?
play tennis?
prefer to go to the beach than the mountains?
would like to live in the country?
would like to live in New York City?
watch more than two hours of television a day?
agree with your parents on political issues?
agree with your parents on most everything?
fight with your brother or sister?
do volunteer work?
would like to do volunteer work?
are in favor of capital punishment?
would like to work in a foreign country?
are trying to conserve energy?
plan to own a Volkswagon some day?
read a lot?

would like to read more?
believe in God?
know what you believe?
wish you knew what you believed?
like yourself?
like the way you look?
are silly?
like to talk on the telephone?
are responsible?
wish you were more responsible?
would like to move to another town or city?
would like to run for office some day?

Just-for-Fun Games

32. Operant Conditioning

This game is based on the theory of positive reinforcement by B.F. Skinner. The object of the game is to make a volunteer do a task without telling that person a word about what he or she is supposed to do. When the volunteer makes a move in the right direction, he or she receives positive reinforcement from the group—in the form of clapping or pounding on a table.

Begin by having the volunteer leave the room. The group decides what task the person should do. For example: the volunteer should walk in the door, over to a Coke bottle, pick it up, and hand it to a designated person. Or, the volunteer should go to a person with a hat on, take it off, and put it on someone else's head.

The tasks can be simple or complicated. Everyone in the group needs to know exactly what the volunteer is supposed to do, so they can reinforce him or her correctly.

Call in the volunteer. The volunteer must figure out what he or she is supposed to do. If the volunteer walks in one direction, and there is no clapping, he/she knows to try another.

No speaking, moaning, or shaking heads. The only sound shold be the clapping and pounding.

This game is funny, sometimes frustrating, but very exciting when the volunteer finally gets it. Gets very loud at that point.

33. Coin Game

This is a good game to use right after supper, if you happen to have long tables set for the meal. This game is best played with two or more long tables placed end to end.

There should be the same number of people on each side of the table. These are the two teams. Team members hold hands with the persons next to them.

The leader stands at the end of the table. Leader flips a coin and covers it with his or her hands. The leader lets the two end people see the coin.

If it is heads, the end people squeeze the hands of the persons next to them. The squeeze is passed all the way down the line.

When it reaches the other end person, he or she stands. The first to stand wins the point.

If it is tails, there is no squeeze. Nothing should happen. No one should stand. If the far end person stands, it is a mistake. The point goes to the other team. The team that reaches eight first wins.

Variation: Rotate end people, so that new people have a chance to start, and new end people to stand. Rotate periodically and make the game fifteen points (or more).

34. Crab Soccer

This game is similar to regular soccer. The object is to get the ball between the goal marks.

Crab soccer is played indoors with a soccer ball. To get into position, the youth sit on the floor and put their hands on the floor behind them. The players move around on their hands and feet.

The ball can be hit with feet, knees, and head, but not hands. Players can collapse on their backs, but they cannot stand up.

Appendix D

Five-Category Index to *Idealog* and *Strategies*

Six of the most highly recommended youth ministry resources are:

Idealog: Creative Ideas for Younger Youth, compiled by Donald B. Schroeder, edited by William Ross Forbes (General Assembly Mission Board, PCUS, 1979).

Idealog: Creative Ideas for Older Youth, compiled by Max Haskett, edited by Guin Tuckett (Christian Board of Publication, 1979).

Strategies for Youth Programs: Junior High/Volumes 1, 2, edited by Barbara A. Withers (Geneva Press, 1978, 1979).

Strategies for Youth Programs: Senior High/Volume 1, edited by Judy R. Fletcher (Geneva Press, 1978); *Volume 2,* edited by Bernie C. Dunphy-Linnartz (1979).

The first two were published for the multidenominational education venture called Christian Education: Shared Approaches (CE:SA).

A big problem for leaders is knowing how to use resources. Any programmatic book is filled with hundreds of ideas and programs. It is hard for category leaders to locate the activities which relate to their categories.

This appendix is an index to these six excellent resources. I have gone through the volumes placing each program, activity, and article in one or more of the five categories used in the leadership team approach.

Leaders: To use this index, simply look for your category. Under each category you will find the appropriate page numbers (activity numbers in *Idealog: Younger Youth*) and a title or a short description. Activities for junior highs are listed first (Idealog, then *Strategies*), followed by those for senior highs.

WORSHIP

Idealog: Younger Youth

Activity 5 — Christmas
        7 — Prayer
       15 — Banners relating to disciples
       17 — Epiphany
       21 — Easter sunrise service and breakfast
       22 — Worship as the early church did
       24 — Lenten family workshop (suggests devotional booklet)
       28 — Psalm 146 (creative expressions for worship)
       43 — Banners on the Beautitudes
       52 — Creating hymns
       56 — Time Capsule (used as dedication in worship)

Strategies: Junior High/Vol. 1

page 24 — Article on planning and leading worship
       69 — Celebration with *joy* as the theme

Strategies: Junior High/Vol. 2

page 168 — Tell Me the Old, Old Story (suggests a closing worship experience)
      170 — I Have a Story to Tell (closing worship)
      171 — A Party with God

Idealog: Older Youth

page 14 — Litany for youth ministry
       16 — Short worship play, "I Am the Lord Your God"
       19 — Short worship play, "Help My Unbelief"
       22 — Worship resource quickies

Strategies: Senior High/Vol. 1

page 11 — Article on spiritual growth
       85 — Create worship on triumphal entry into
            Jerusalem
    121 — Mini-meditation on sin and forgiveness

Strategies: Senior High/Vol. 2

page 14 — Seasons of Celebration . . . the Church Year
            (article)
    23 — Spirituality and Life (article)
    27 — Liturgy and Ritual (articie)
  118 — Re-confessing . . . an Activity of Worship,
            Reflection, and Confession
  124 — Re-affirmation . . . and Personal Sacraments
  145 — Understanding and Celebrating Significant
            Transitions

STUDY

Idealog: Younger Youth

Activity 2 — Death
        3 — Darkness/trust exercise
        4 — All about Jesus
        5 — Advent/Christmas
        6 — Advent/Christmas
        7 — Prayer
        9 — Growing up
    11 — Affirmation of selves
    14 — Christmas

15 — The twelve disciples
16 — Christmas
19 — Study of other denominations by working
     with another denomination's youth group
24 — Lent (with emphasis on families)
25 — Making a film
28 — Psalm 146
29 — Careers
30 — Tasks of a minister
31 — Study of words (justice, love, hope, etc.) in
     Scripture
33 — Study of books of the Bible
34 — Game on church history
36 — Junk art night
37 — Parents
38 — Places your church is engaged in mission
39 — Identity—A Name to Remember
40 — Choices of names for people and places
41 — Development of the Bible
42 — Jesus' life
43 — The Beautitudes
45 — What it means to be ''in''
49 — Charades on biblical personalities
50 — Values auction
51 — Bible skills by C.B.
52 — Hymn writing
53 — Jesus' entry into Jerusalem
54 — Third world countries
56 — A Time Capsule (identity)
57 — Christian symbols
58 — Authority of the Bible
59 — Inspiration of the Bible

60 — Faith/commitment
61 — Nature
63 — God is . . .
64 — The church year

Strategies: Junior High/Vol. 1
page 52 — Issues concerning junior highs
55 — The church
59 — Leadership
63 — Identity: growing up
73 — Loneliness
75 — Identity: being different or unique
79 — Identity: hassles, hopes, hang-ups, help, home, happiness
81 — Community: relationships, caring, sharing
85 — Communication: listening skills
88 — Friendship
94 — Simulation game on spending money
96 — Power
99 — Values
104 — Faith, Jesus-style
106 — What do I believe?
109 — Issues in today's society
112 — Freedom vs. family
116 — The Last Supper
118 — Self-expression
121 — Making decisions
124 — Television
128 — Advertising
131 — Communicating/opportunities for service in the community
134 — Death
138 — Families
141 — Relating to the opposite sex
144 — What's a handicap?
147 — Seeing
150 — Simulation game on use of money
154 — Winning
162 — Use of the senses in worship
165 — Wonder/prayer
170 — Christmas/ways of celebrating birthdays

Strategies: Junior High/Vol. 2
page 38 — Mirror, Mirror on the Wall . . . I'm Changing
42 — Dealing with Changes in Our Bodies
45 — Top Dog . . . Underdog
50 — Family (involves parents)
54 — Evil
56 — What's Bugging Us?
58 — Getting Our Heads Straight
60 — Big Bad Wolves (images)
63 — Values
67 — Decision making
73 — Heroes
77 — Crimes
79 — Peer pressure
82 — Relationships
85 — Faith journeys
88 — Wholeness
96–106 — Me and My Life Cycle (six sessions)
108 — Supporting struggles toward independence
112 — Identity

115 — Lonely or Alone or Both
120 — Newcomers
123 — Rejection
126 — Self-esteem
134 — Drugs
137 — Decision making
141 — Buying Power
145 — Enabling youth to plan and do serving projects
150 — Sex roles
153 — Looking for Adventure
156 — Our Media Parent: TV
159 — Restrictions, limitations
163 — Celebrating Advent, Christmas, Epiphany
165 — Observing Lent, Easter, Pentecost
167 — Stories of those who knew Jesus
169 — I Have a Story to Tell . . .

Idealog: Older Youth
page 28C — 24-Hour Hunger Lock-in
49 — Six sessions on *Feelings* (Guilt, The Family Gap, Male/Female Role Reversal, Love Machines, Paint Emotions, Wearing Labels)
56 — Three sessions on *Values* (Value Strategies, What Are the World's Values?, Values Auction)
59 — Four sessions on *Relating to Others* (What Is Communication?, The Masks We Wear, The Generation Gap, Friendship and Sexuality)
63 — Five sessions on *Religious Growth* (Prayer, Expressing the Faith, Exercise in Christian Discipleship, The Twelve Disciples, A Church Membership Game)
72 — Two sessions on *Education* (Choosing a College, Choosing Not to Go to College)
74 — Two sessions on *Holidays* (Christmas Test— biblical knowledge, Banners for the Twelve— Easter)
77 — Multimedia Bible Study
77 — New Testament Images of the Church
78 — What Is a Steward?
79 — Six Studies in Galatians
86 — Program quickie on The Law and Youth

Strategies: Senior High/Vol. 1
page 14 — Simulation game on the Presbyterian process of church government
24 — Mission Midway
32 — Hunger
39 — Relationships/listening
43 — Power
46 — Setting One Another Free
50 — Hunger
53 — Love, loving, and the "unlovable"
57 — Being Family
61 — Beliefs/Apostles' Creed
65 — Creating your own religion
70 — Claiming our gifts and talents (identity)
74 — Creator, creation/humanity
79 — Identifying and affirming our talents and gifts
83 — Expressing ideas through a variety of media
85 — Bible study—Jesus' entry into Jerusalem
89 — Living simply
96 — Exploring the meaning of names
100 — Sex roles and discrimination

104 — Careers/vocations
107 — Identity—present and future
111 — A Christian path to creative decisions
114 — Decision-making/responsibility
118 — Prayer
121 — Sin and forgiveness
124 — Forgiveness
127 — Communication (parents and youth)
130 — Awareness of older persons
133 — Combining two racially different groups for getting acquainted, recreation, and discussion
138 — Cain and Abel
140 — Tower of Babel
143 — Noah
146 — Noah's rainbow
149 — Abraham and Isaac (freedom to respond)
152 — Jacob and Esau (broken relationships)
156 — Slavery and breaking free
159 — Moses (risking love)
162 — Expressing hope in hard times
166 — Three programs on the Ten Commandments
175 — The golden calf (what it is today)

Strategies: Senior High/Vol. 2

page 14 — Seasons of the Church Year (article)
      23 — Spirituality and Life (article)
      27 — Liturgy and Ritual (article)
      30 — Image of God
      33 — Understanding God in Christ as coming into our personal and community lives
      36 — On God
      39 — Pioneers of the Kingdom
      43 — Superpersons (special people)
      45 — Discipline and Discipleship
      48 — Dating
      51 — Becoming Affirming Reformers
      54 — Be-Attitudes
      61 — World religions
      66 — Suicide
      69 — If-ness of the Future
      73 — Exploring oppression and liberation
      77 — Identifying with the needs of our human brothers and sisters
      82 — Pain
      87 — Sexist language and God talk
      90 — Violence
      99 — Hunger
     102 — Dreams and lifestyles for the future
     105 — Leavetaking
     109 — Leaving parents
     112 — Letting go
     115 — Re-deciding . . . the Face of Jesus
     118 — Re-confessing
     124 — Re-affirmation
     126 — Re-calling
     129 — Vocation
     132 — Vocation
     138 — Vocation
     145 — Where Do I Go from Here?
     150 — Imagining—Dreaming—Wow!
     155 — Rites and rituals
     159 — Ritual Writing

163 — Broken homes
167 — An Experience with Hospice/death and dying
172 — Article on death
174 — Article on cult and church
178 — Pseudo-religious Cults (article)

MINISTRY WITHIN THE CONGREGATION

Idealog: Younger Youth

Activity 8 — Session for youth and church officers
         12 — Activities with older adults
         13 — Work projects around the church
         16 — Making chrismon tree for church
         18 — Caroling
         21 — Easter sunrise service and breakfast
         23 — Tutoring with children
         24 — Lenten family workshop
         25 — Make film on the church
         26 — Halloween party for children of the church
         30 — What the minister does
         32 — Educating the congregation on hunger
         38 — Where your church is involved in mission
         46 — Old Flick Night
         48 — Mission—church work as vocation

Strategies: Junior High/Vol. 2

page 50 — Adult/youth session on roles
     86 — Use of film, "Pilgrim's Adventure"
    110 — Parent/youth get-together

Idealog: Older Youth

page 27 — Songfest
     28 — Amateur talent night
     28A — Donated painting (cleanup, fix up)
     29D — A Young-Old "Trough" (ice cream party)
     29F — Thank-you party for church school teachers and adult leaders
     30I — Taxi service for shut-ins and the elderly
     30J — Halloween carnival
     41 — Work day
     70 — Ministry to shut-ins
     71 — Adopt a grandparent
     71 — Entertain senior citizens
     86G — Encountering young children

Strategies: Senior High/Vol. 1

page 24 — Mission Midway (stewardship)
      50 — Hunger (letter to our congregation)
      70 — Sharing gifts and talents with congregation
      74 — A sketch on creation/Creator
      79 — Share talents with the congregation
     127 — Parent and youth meeting (on communication)
     130 — Youth and older persons

Strategies: Senior High/Vol. 2

page 97 — Discovering ways to be involved in the congregation

SERVICE

Idealog: Younger Youth

Activity 12 — Ministering to elderly in nursing homes
16 — Making chrismon tree for nursing home or hospital
18 — Caroling
26 — Halloween party at hospital, children's homes, etc.
44 — Sharing talents with elderly in nursing homes
48 — Ambassadors in Mission (learning about missions)
54 — Third world countries

Strategies: Junior High/Vol. 1

page 96 — Power/decision-making/introduction to service to the community
109 — Getting involved in issues
131 — Opportunities for service/introduction to service to the community

Strategies: Junior High/Vol. 2

page 17 — Don't Forget the World (article)
28 — Mission Is Possible (article)
145 — Enabling youth to plan and do serving projects

Idealog: Older Youth

page 28 — Painting, cleanup, fix up (children's home, day care center, senior center)
28B — Lord's Acre Project (garden-grown food sharing)
28C — 24-hour hunger lock-in
29G — Repair toys for Christmas (needy children)
30H — Christmas trees for elderly
30I — Taxi service for shut-ins and elderly
41 — Work day (proceeds go to service project)
70 — Ministry to shut-ins
71 — Adopt a grandparent
71 — Entertain senior citizens

Strategies: Senior High/Vol. 1

page 32 — Starve-in (responding to world hunger)
50 — Poverty/hunger
79 — Sharing talents and gifts with others
130 — Youth becoming aware of older persons (a preface to service projects with older adults)

Strategies: Senior High/Vol. 2

page 95 — Enabling youth to plan and do serving projects
97 — Beyond Ourselves
99 — Hunger
102 — Turning dreams into a reality

FELLOWSHIP

Idealog: Younger Youth

Activity 1 — Make your own yearbook
         3 — Experiencing darkness
         9 — Growing up
        10 — Creating activities and exploring issues and concerns of junior highs
        11 — Group builder on affirmation
        20 — Let's get acquainted
        27 — Planning
        35 — Getting together with another youth group by tape
        40 — Identifying names
        47 — Sharing studies and projects at a meeting of many youth groups
        55 — Fix up "a place for us"
        62 — Worship lock-in

Strategies: Junior High/Vol. 1

page 27 — Article on using games with junior highs (a few games)
      34 — Article on retreats
      46 — A session of group-building activities
      50 — Exercises in group building, communicating, trusting
      52 — Identifying issues facing junior highs
      59 — Being a leader, decision making
      63 — Identity/growing
      67 — Three games (British Bulldog, Midnight Football, Barnyard Game)
     160 — Creating new games
     174 — Celebrating "our group"
     177 — Celebrating and saying good-bye to the group

Strategies: Junior High/Vol. 2

page 33 — Uses of Play (article)
      91 — All They Want to Do Is Play

      94 — Play Places
     132 — PUDWOP
     171 — A Party with God

Idealog: Older Youth

page 25A — Taking and using photos of the group
     25B — What's our group like?
     25C — Ways to recruit kids to the group
     28C — Hunger lock-in
     29E — Paint the youth room
     32 — New style of youth ministry
     33 — The Friendship Web (team building, close of retreat)
     33 — Cooperation or Competition?
     34 — Youth Alive Retreat
     36 — Art by Committee
     37 — Four quickie group processes
     39 — Five recreation quickies (Earth Ball Game, "I'm Like a —," Adverbs, Ho-Ho-Ho, Situation)
     40 — Balloon theater
     42 — Suggestions for socials
     44 — How to plan for a trip
     45 — Trip and outing quickies
     47 — Rafting
     48 — Experience in self-discovery
     84 — Six program quickies (50-Foot Hike, Futures, Make Something, Olympics, Using Local Resources, Law and Youth)

Strategies: Senior High/Vol. 1

page 67 — Opportunities for exploring ecumenical youth ministries
     133 — Two groups, racially different, meet together

Strategies: Senior High/Vol. 2

page 59 — Retreat/charge
     155 — Rituals
     159 — Ritual Writing

Notes

Chapter 1

1. Lyle E. Schaller, *Assimilating New Members* (Nashville: Abingdon Press, 1978), p. 77.

Chapter 2

1. John H. Westerhoff, III, *Will Our Children Have Faith?* (New York: Seabury Press, 1976), p. 94.
2. *A Declaration of Faith*, PCUS, ch. 7 (1).
3. Hans Kung, *On Being a Christian* (New York: Doubleday, 1976), p. 478.
4. *Will Our Children Have Faith?* pp. 22-23.
5. Ibid., p. 44.
6. Thank you, John Westerhoff, for this approach to confirmation commissioning.

Appendix C

1. Lyman Coleman, *Serendipity* (Waco, Texas: Word, Inc., 1972), pp. 27-28.
2. Lyman Coleman, *Groups in Action* (Word, Inc.: 1972), p. 26.
3. Lyman Coleman, *Encyclopedia of Serendipity* (Colorado Springs: Serendipity House, 1976), p. 51.
4. Lyman Coleman, *Breaking Free* (Word, Inc.: 1971), pp. 26-27.
5. Helen & Larry Eisenberg, *The Omnibus of Fun* (New York: Association Press, 1956), p. 347.
6. *Encyclopedia of Serendipity*, p. 54.
7. Lyman Coleman, *Handbook of Serendipity* (Serendipity House, 1976), p. 46.
8. Adapted from a Lyman Coleman exercise.
9. *Handbook of Serendipity*, p. 52.

Index

Adolescents: characteristics of, 19, 23–24, 39, 45, 46, 57–60, 86, 90, 91, 101–102, 103, 105, 107; resources on, 60, 112–113

Adult involvement in youth ministry, 11, 14–16, 31–32, 38–40, 46–47, 52, 62, 63, 66, 91

advisors, 10–11, 13–15, 16, 17–18, 19, 23, 24, 25–26, 27, 29, 30, 34, 35–47, 48, 69–70, 89, 93; leadership styles of, 17, 107, 109; qualities of, 36–38, 50; relationship with youth, 13–14, 16–18, 31–32, 36–40; responsibilities of, 38–47, 67, 68, 84–86, 98, 102, 107–108; resources on, 112–113

Advocates for youth ministry, 16, 46–47, 85–86, 91

Age group characteristics. See Adolescents, characteristics of

"Animals," 130

Assimilating New Members (Lyle Schaller), 15

Authority figure, 13, 23, 36, 106. See also Discipline

"A What?" 76, 77, 127–128

Bannerman, Glenn, and Fakkema, Bob, *Guide for Recreation Leaders,* 78, 113

Barth, Karl, 20

Bible study, 19, 23, 40, 77, 111; resources for, 115

Bulletin boards, 84

Calendar, 11–12, 17, 26, 28–30, 31–32, 33, 42, 49, 65–66, 71, 74–75, 80–82, 83, 91, 93–94; illustrations, 12, 71, 82

Campus Crusade, 19–20

Canceling activities, 38

"Can't Say No," 126

Choir directors, 91

Church, 19–24

Church membership, 19

Church school, 17, 20–22, 24, 29, 38, 86, 89, 91; curriculum, 23, 86, 91; resources for, 112–115

Church school teachers, 17, 20, 24, 29, 38, 40, 48, 89, 91

Cliques, 40, 76, 91–92

Clown ministry, 117

"Coin Game," 63, 66, 133

Coleman, Lyman, *Serendipity* series, 114, 125

Combining junior and senior highs, 90

Commitment: of leaders, 14, 16, 24, 36, 49; of youth, 24, 107

Communicating youth ministry to the congregation, 26, 29, 30, 46–47, 83–87, 102, 104, 107

Community building. See Group building

Community of faith. See Church

Confirmation/commissioning, 23–24

Cookout: orientation, 54; youth/leader, 54, 60–61, 69

Coordinators, 11, 16, 26, 27; responsibilities of, 18, 28–34, 39, 42, 48, 54–55, 60–61, 64–67, 68–71, 78, 79, 80–81, 83, 85–86, 93, 98, 101, 103–105, 110–111

Corbett, Jan, *Creative Youth Leadership,* 105, 111, 112; *Explore: Vol. 1,* 114; *Respond: Vol. 2,* 114

Couples as leaders, 52

"Crab Soccer," 77, 133

Creative Youth Leadership (Jan Corbett), 60, 105, 110, 112

Culture: effect on youth, 23, 58, 106–107

D.C.E. (director of Christian education), 18, 25, 30, 35, 40, 48, 80, 84

Declaration of Faith, A (Proposed Book of Confessions), 20

Devotions: resources for, 115–116

Discipline, 13–14, 36, 38, 46, 78

District. See Presbytery/district

Drama: resources for, 116

Ecumenical possibilities, 90–91

Evaluation, 30, 33, 40, 43–45, 61, 79, 81, 87, 92, 93; questions for, 44–45, 87

Explore: Volume 1 (Jan Corbett), 114

Exuberant Years, The (Ginny Ward Holderness), 10, 35, 68, 105, 110, 112, 118–119

Failure, 101, 102

Faith development, 19, 23, 30; resource on, 113 (no. 17)

Fakkema, Bob, and Bannerman, Glenn, *Guide for Recreation Leaders,* 78, 113

Fellowship, 19, 64, 91; as category, 1, 2, 37, 40–41, 49, 52, 56, 73–75; resources for, 112–115, (nos. 3, 15, 16, 20–43), 116–117, 124
Fellowship of Christian Athletes, 19
Five categories of youth ministry, 10, 11, 27, 40–42, 49, 56, 61, 64–65, 69, 70, 73, 89–90, 118, 120–124
Fluegelman, Andrew, *The New Games Book: Play Hard, Play Fair, Nobody Hurt*, 78, 113
Follow-up meeting. *See* Planning retreat, follow-up to
Forbes, William R., *Presbyterian Youth Ministries: Youth Manual*, 105, 112
"Four Facts/One Lie," 61, 76, 77, 105, 129

Goal setting, 10, 11, 18, 20, 50–51, 70, 73, 84, 94–95, 103, 106, 107, 118–119
"Grand Prix Races," 76, 77, 128
Group building, 31, 40, 54, 60–61, 68, 80, 125–133; resource for, 114 (no. 36)
"Guess Who?" 77, 129
Guest speakers, 32–33
Guide for Recreation Leaders (Glenn Bannerman and Bob Fakkema), 78, 113

Handbell choir director, 91
"How Many of You. . . ?" 63, 66, 131

Identity formation, 19, 23
"In Event of Fire," 129
Intergenerational activity, 13, 22, 23, 86
"Introduction Interview," 54, 61, 76, 125–126

"John, John, John," 76, 126
Junior highs, 36, 57–60, 63, 65–66, 90, 119; combining junior and senior high groups, 90; junior high school teachers, 91; resources for, 112–114 (nos. 9–12, 22, 24, 27–29)

Küng, Hans, *On Being a Christian*, 20

Large church, 88, 91–92
Leaders. *See* Advisors
Leadership roles among youth, 30, 42–46, 54–55, 66, 68, 83, 91–92, 94, 98–102
Leadership styles, 17, 103, 107, 109
Leadership team, 11, 14, 30, 44, 46–47, 91; team building, 103, 105, 106, 109–110
Leadership training, 11, 14, 15–16, 30, 38, 47, 54–55, 62, 68, 69, 78, 93, 103–111
Lifestyle, 24; resources on, 115 (nos. 45, 46)
Lock-in, 17

"Machines," 127
Magazines/periodicals, 117
Media, 78–79, 84, 86; resources on, 78, 117
Methods, 30, 38, 44, 110–111; resources on, 212 (nos. 2–4), 113 (nos. 13, 14, 16), 115 (nos. 14–44)
"Mingle," 127

Mini-courses, 45, 90, 121–122
Minister, 18, 25–26, 30, 35–36, 40, 47, 48, 69, 80, 84
Ministry Within the Congregation, 10, 11, 21, 37, 40, 41, 48, 49, 52, 56, 69, 73–75, 89, 90; resources for, 113–116 (nos. 22–34), 45, 46, 61, 62, 122–123
Mission of the church, 20–22; resource on, 113 (no. 18)
"More Hamburger than Steak," 63, 66, 131
Motivation: of youth, 16–17, 38, 42–43, 44–46, 91–92, 98–101, 102, 103

"Name Charade," 76, 77, 127
Name tags, 70, 71–72, 126; descriptive, 126; Name Anagrams, 126; Name Tag Collage, 126; Name Tag Symbols, 126
Nelson, Virgil and Lynn, *Retreat Handbook*, 75, 78, 113
New Games Book: Play Hard, Play Fair, Nobody Hurt (Andrew Fluegelman, ed.), 78, 113
New members, 14–15, 16
Newsletter, 83
Ng, David, *Youth: A Manual for CE:SA*, 105, 110, 112

Officers, 91–92
On Being a Christian (Hans Küng), 20
"One Frog," 76, 77, 128
"Open-ended Statements," 61, 76, 77, 129
"Operant Conditioning," 76, 77, 132
Orientation cookout, 54–55

Parachurch groups, 19–20
Parent Night, 55, 61, 62–67, 81, 103, 110
Parents, 18, 23, 25, 29–31, 34, 47, 60, 62–67, 103, 106, 107; as leaders, 48, 52; involvement of, 30, 81, 86, 110
Peers, 19, 23, 60, 106, 107
Periodicals/magazines, 117
Planning, 11, 27, 28–29, 30, 31, 40, 41–43, 46, 54–56, 68–75, 90, 103, 119; resources for, 112–113
Planning process, 40–43, 54–56, 70–75, 118–119
Planning retreat, 11, 12, 31, 40–42, 54–56, 61, 65, 68–79, 89, 91, 92, 94, 103, 119; follow-up to, 11, 31, 41, 65, 75, 80–82
Policy-making board, 18, 23, 25, 27, 29, 36, 40, 84, 85–86, 102
Prayer: resources on, 115–116
Prejudice, 60
Presbyterian Youth Ministries: Youth Manual (compiled by Jill Senior, ed. by Wm. R. Forbes), 60, 105, 112
Presbytery/district, 30, 32, 47, 71, 74, 83, 86
Program planning. *See* Planning
Publicity, 31, 38, 47, 83–84, 92, 107

Recreation, 40, 61, 71, 76–77, 78, 124, 125, 126–129, 132–133; resources on, 113 (nos. 19–21)
Recruiting, 14–15, 16, 25, 27, 29, 33, 48–52, 54, 89, 91, 93
Resource persons, 32–33, 93, 103, 104
Resources, 30, 32–33, 47, 110–111, 112–117, 120–124
Respond: Volume 2 (Jan Corbett), 114
Responsible persons, 11, 30, 33, 38, 42–44, 44–45, 54–55, 64, 73, 75, 80–81, 83, 84, 91–92, 94, 99–102, 103
Retreat Handbook (Virgil and Lynn Nelson), 75, 78, 113
Retreats, 68–69, 75–79; resource on, 113 (no. 19)

Schaller, Lyle, *Assimilating New Members,* 15
School, 23, 58, 91, 106–107
Scout leaders, 91
Senior highs, 36, 57–60, 63, 66, 90, 119; combining with junior highs, 90; resources for, 112–115 (nos. 1–8, 15–16, 23, 25, 26, 30–40); school teachers of, 91
Senior, Jill, *Presbyterian Youth Ministries: Youth Manual,* 60, 105, 112
Serendipity series (Lyman Coleman), 114, 125
Service, 10, 11, 21, 37, 40, 41, 49, 56, 73–75, 89, 90, 123–124; resources for, 113–115 (nos. 16, 22–34, 45, 46)
Session. *See* Policy-making board
Sex, sexuality, 60
"Sign My Card," 66, 127
"Simple Introductions," 126
Small church, 13, 17, 88–90; resource for, 112 (no. 5)
Small groups: as method, 40, 63–64, 78–79, 90, 111, 129–130
Songbooks, 116
"Songs" (game), 130
"Special Dinner, A," 77, 129
"Stand on Numbers," 63, 66, 130
"Stranded on an Island," 129
Study, 10, 11, 21, 37, 40–41, 49–50, 56, 64, 73–75, 90–91, 121–122; resources for, 113–115 (nos. 16, 22–46)
Sunday night, 10, 11, 17, 18, 19, 27, 30, 34, 44, 49, 52, 73–74, 80, 91, 98, 99; resources for, 112–115, 120–124
Sunday school. *See* Church school

Test churches, 5, 18
Theology of youth ministry, 19–24, 103, 107
"Think of . . . ," 130

Values, 23, 24, 60; value-related exercises, 130–132; resource on, 114 (no. 36)
"Virginia Reel Conversation," 54, 66, 71, 72–73, 130
Visits, 49
Volunteers, 16, 51

Westerhoff, John, *Will Our Children Have Faith?* 19, 20–21
"Who Am I?" 66, 127, 130
Will Our Children Have Faith? (John Westerhoff), 19, 20–21
Worship, 10, 11, 19, 21, 37, 40, 41, 49, 56, 73–75, 76–79, 90, 91, 120; resources for, 113–116 (nos. 15, 22–34, 40, 45–69)

Young Life, 19–20
Youth: involvement in ministry and life of the church, 10, 13 15–16, 17, 19–22, 26–27, 30, 38, 40, 91–92, 102, 120–124; leadership roles (*see* Leadership roles among youth); relationship with advisors (*see* Advisors, relationship with youth); visibility of, 13, 15–16, 84–85, 86
Youth advisors. *See* Advisors
Youth: A Manual for CE:SA (Dave Ng), 105, 110, 112
Youth choir directors, 91
Youth council, 26, 91–92
Youth director, 25–26, 48, 88
Youth division chairperson, 48
Youth/leader cookout, 54, 60–61, 69
Youth leaders. *See* Advisors
Youth ministry workshop, 86, 102, 104–105

"Zip, Zap," 76, 126